Becoming A Novice Yogi

Meditations on Recovery from Mental Illness

Elizabeth Owen

Cover design: Nicki Averill Design
Typesetting: Clockwork Graphic Design
Printed in Australia by Griffin Press Printing Pty Ltd
Published by Peritia Press

I've graduated from taking to giving

Dedication

For my fellow kindred spirit, River Hill, who encourages me to be a better version of myself and for making me believe that I have a story worth sharing.

Acknowledgements

I would like to thank Stephen Adrian, my good friend, for his support. He has seen me at my worst and nurtured me through those terrible times. Today, we are best friends. Thank you for being yourself and sharing your ideas with me. You were my bedrock when my mind was at its most fragile.

To my sister, Julie Owen-Matthews, for maintaining a lifelong relationship, despite living at opposite ends of the world.

I would also like to thank Sadhguru, who has touched the lives of millions of people through his yoga practices, Inner Engineering, and Isha Kriya. His wisdom and presence in this world has affected me deeply and I consider it an honour to have touched his feet. I am forever devoted to him, my guru.

To the readers of this book. Wherever you are along the path, know that there is hope after mental illness. There is not only hope but there is a real chance of creating equilibrium in your life. Finding joy is possible again. This book is for you, written with heart, and with the intention of easing your pain and suffering. So be it.

Disclaimer

This book is not an alternative method for treating mental illness. If you suspect you have an illness, it is recommended that you seek professional help immediately. Do not try to resolve your mental illness alone. There are plenty of professionals who understand the devastating impacts of mental illness and can provide help.

Also, never underestimate the power of friendships and those who are close to you at this moment in time. Reach out and communicate – you may be surprised by the love and support you already have around you.

Table of Contents

Introduction

"Don't keep any corner of your existence away from divinity.

The divine should be interwoven into every aspect of your life."

Gurudev Sri Sri Ravi Shankar

This book is about re-framing the narratives we tell ourselves. In sharing my story, I hope to show that it is possible, and indeed necessary, to reframe your story. People's capacity for suffering is enormous if left unchecked. I am a testament to that fact. Yet, despite the turmoil and troubles in my life, I have restructured my narrative to be more in line with my truth.

Are you living by an out-dated frame of reference? Do you need help in rewriting your story to be more in line with your truth? Maybe, by reading my story, you can learn a little more about how to stand in your own truth.

Ever since I was a child, I split myself off from reality. It's been an unsafe world in which I've lived. People have hurt me, and I've put up barriers to protect myself. However, in putting up the barriers, I cut myself off from the inclusive emotions of love. I barricaded myself into the prison of my mind, and remained there for the majority of my life.

It's been a long, hard road, but I am now blessed. My blessing is that I am filled with love. It feels as though I am attuned to a higher purpose. I am a child of the divine.

I have arrived at the warm sunlight at the end of a long road. I would like to help show you the path to the sunlight.

Reaching The Destination With A Trusted Friend

For those of you who have been diagnosed with mental illness, I have walked in your shoes. Twelve years ago, I was in pretty bad shape. After years of suffering, I was diagnosed with schizoaffective disorder. This is a combination of schizophrenia and bipolar. It has symptoms of overwhelming depressive lows, manic euphoric highs, delusions, and hallucinations. I spent months on the secure wards of several different hospitals. As my illness had crept up on me, one painful day at a time, over many years, I didn't think I was ill, and so my progress with treatment was slow.

I had been unhappy for a very long time. I was a loner, spending most of my time at home. I hadn't had a regular job for years and was estranged from my family. I had recently returned to university to do a Masters of Education when the stress became too much. I started emailing a lecturer about how I felt – disconnected – and couldn't stop pouring out my thoughts and emotions.

It was like a floodgate had opened after so many years in isolation. My suffering flowed out in one long continuous stream of frantic emails. Looking back, I wouldn't do anything differently. I needed to confide in someone and I am glad it was my lecturer. He didn't quite know what to do with me but he did actively listen to my pain, and that was all I needed. However, it was the beginning of a downward spiral. I spent night after night sobbing in the bath. My body was in physical pain with tremendous tension and my mind wouldn't stop racing. My emotions were chaotic. I felt I couldn't talk with Stephen. It was all too intense.

At the time, I was reading a book called *A Course in Miracles*. It was a surreal perspective on the world, which turned my beliefs upside down. What I had thought was real suddenly seemed to be devoid of meaning. Small day-to-day accomplishments, such as taking a shower or getting dressed, had become major challenges. I hardly ate and lost a lot of weight. At my lowest point, I weighed just forty-five kilos.

It has taken me several years to regain a measure of control over my life. I have had relapses along the way. I do not see myself as fully healed. I am still on the path. However, my emotions and thoughts have calmed, and I am now actively engaged in meditation on a daily basis, which helps me to retain balance. The years of recovery have sometimes been a long haul up a steep mountain. At other times, it has felt as though everything has clicked into place and been an easy freewheeling downhill run.

No one can fully articulate the depth of pain a soul can feel when dealing with mental illness. There is no other pain quite like it. Those of us who have been there feel each other's pain. We know the terrain.

When we experience mental illness it can be difficult to recognise how deeply immersed in our pain we are until after the event. It is only once we recover and look back that we can see what a dark, desolate place we were in.

How do we transform our suffering? How did I transform mine? By taking things one day at a time and, through meditation, developing a gentle acceptance of my current situation and letting go of the past. With time, I was also able to let go of the future, so that I could concentrate on my breathing, focusing my attention on my body, my emotions, and my thoughts, slowly letting the body's tension relax, letting the emotions be deeply felt, and letting the thoughts 'ungrasp' themselves.

Transforming insanity can be a simple process or it can be as complicated as we want to make it. If you have acute or chronic symptoms, then seeing a doctor is a must. Medication corrects the biological chemistry in the body, which is a necessity before any further healing can occur.

Blistered Childhood Memories

My childhood was filled with hatred, anger, and jealousy. I grew up in a domestically violent household. Ever since I can remember I was frightened of the people around me. Those who were meant to nurture, love, and protect me did the opposite. I was sexually abused and beaten from a young age. It wasn't just me – my mother, brothers, and sister were beaten too. I used to hate the beatings with the belt that had the steel buckle - always across the back of the legs where the skin is the most tender, and easily covered to hide the bruises.

When I was six, I stole fifty dollars from under the mattress in my mother's bedroom. The money was from my stepfather's pay packet. I went to the shops and bought cigarettes and a box of chocolates. I told the shopkeeper to keep the change. My friend and I then went to the park, sat on the grass, ate all the chocolates and tried smoking the cigarettes. They tasted foul. Coughing and spluttering, we threw them away.

My stepfather accused my mother of stealing the money and gave her a beating. I felt guilty, but was too scared to own up for fear of what he would do to me. Later that night, the shopkeeper knocked on the door and explained to my mother what I had done.

I was eating my mother's delicious lamb stew in the living room, precariously balancing the soup bowl on the arm of the sofa, when the shopkeeper came to the door. I could hear the muffled conversation, then my stepfather's angry, forceful voice. I still remember the terror of the beating he gave me. That night left a deep scar in my mind, mainly because I believed I deserved the beating.

There are many scars from childhood. The physical violence was only a small part of it. For me, the verbal abuse was far worse. Being told every day that I was a worthless bastard left a much deeper wound – one that didn't fade like the bruises.

I used to wet the bed when I was a young child - a habit that continued into my early teenage years. I was afraid to get up in the middle of the night and go to the toilet, in case I bumped into my stepfather. Sleeping in a wet bed was a horrible experience, especially in winter when the sheets used to be ice cold. My mother wouldn't wash the sheets for months at a time, so I would have to lie in a permanently wet bed with a wet mattress.

My bedroom was next to the bathroom. The partition between the bedroom and the bathroom was wafer thin. I shared the room with my older brother, Kevin, the youngest of the boys, and just a year older than me. We had bunk beds, and from my bunk I could hear every sound when someone was in the toilet at night. My stepfather had a hacking cough from the cigarettes he smoked, and would bring up phlegm which he would then spit loudly into the toilet bowl. He always made so much noise peeing and shitting. I could even hear him crinkling the paper to wipe himself. We couldn't afford to buy toilet paper so we had folded up squares of newspaper instead. I hated the feel of the newspaper. It always left a black print on my hands.

When I was fourteen, my mother moved out of the house we shared with my stepfather. She couldn't take his violence and abuse anymore. We were given a house in Heol Cadifor, Penlan, in Wales. I had my own bedroom, the three boys shared a room, and my mother and Helen slept in the third bedroom.

After a couple of months in the house things were going well. There wasn't the heavy atmosphere that my stepfather created, where we would be walking on eggshells, never knowing if he was going to explode at any moment.

We were all in the kitchen one day when my mother dropped the bombshell. She was going to go back and live with my stepfather. The second bombshell was that she was only taking Helen with her. I didn't know whether to feel relieved or devastated. I was shattered that my mother was abandoning me. She was leaving me in the care of my eldest brother, Stephen, whom I feared terribly. He was a big, muscular man with a violent temper.

So, by the time I was fourteen I'd been abandoned by both my parents. The night my mother told us she was leaving, I decided to end my life. The pain was too great for me. I felt desolate. I couldn't talk with anyone - there was no one around who I trusted or loved. I took the box of headache tablets from the kitchen cupboard and, in the privacy of my bedroom, I swallowed them all.

I woke up in the middle of the night and was

violently sick, alone in my room. My attempt at suicide had failed. I felt even worse than before. I hated life, and I hated the violence and misery that was in it.

My late teens and early twenties were a blur of jobs I disliked during the week, and drinking heavily every weekend. I drank copious amounts of alcohol, to dull the noise in my head and to stop the feelings of loneliness and despair. One weekend, I visited a work colleague at her house, and met her brother, Phil – the Dubliner. We clicked straight away and started dating immediately.

In February 1992, we emigrated to Sydney. We arrived at the height of summer. It was hot and humid, and I loved it! It was as if I had arrived home. Oh to be young, in love, and in paradise! I thought I had it made. I saw Australia as an opportunity to make a fresh start, whereas Phil was happy to carry on living the same lifestyle we'd had in London, working through the week and drinking heavily every weekend. We started to argue more and more, until I finally decided to leave him. In the end, my decision was mostly based on the way we disrespected each other. I didn't like it, and was aware that I was the main culprit. I didn't know how to express myself or how to calmly have a conversation about our differences, and so I was aggressive towards him. I didn't like the way I was communicating, but I didn't have the tools to behave otherwise.

The main friendship in my life, and the longest to date, is the friendship I have with Stephen, who I've known for twenty-six years. I know that without him by my side I would have ended up dead long ago. He has been my rock during tough times and has been the stable one in our friendship when my emotions were scattered. I owe him so much.

I have grown as a person since meeting Stephen, becoming more emotionally and mentally stable, despite having had a major breakdown twelve years ago. Stephen has smoothed off my rough edges. We rarely argue and, if we do, it is civilised and neither of us attacks the other person. There aren't many things that I dislike about Stephen. I like his stability. He rarely has moods. He's intelligent and can talk for hours which suits me fine, because I don't like to talk too much at home. I prefer to listen.

We have grown together as friends over the years. I have learnt the art of friendship through studying my reactions to him. We've been through rough patches, particularly when I became ill. I left him for a while, but quickly realised how much I missed him. Through my illness and recovery, I've developed much more of an appreciation of him, and myself, and the closeness of our long-term relationship. There's deep value in having someone know you for a long time, you don't have to explain your life to someone, they know you and share your history. The same is true of the relationship I have with my sister, Julie.

***

Growing up, my mind was like a derelict, haunted log cabin in the wilderness, surrounded by a dark and dangerous forest. I was afraid of my own shadow, and that of anyone else who came near me. Twelve years ago, I had a complete and total mental breakdown. The hauntings of the past caught up with me, and my log cabin went up in smoke, leaving me internally homeless. I was totally broken. The only thing that kept me going was meditation.

In meditation, I could look at my mind. I could remove the layers and explore my emotions. I came closer to the fear, anger, and hatred that I was exposed to as a child. I learned how to be a little calmer in the face of the destructive feelings that lived inside me.

I've been meditating for twenty-six years. Over this time, I've dismantled my mind piece-by-piece, and grown to appreciate the nuances of my thoughts and emotions. I nurture them. I have created a new internal home for myself. Not a haunted dwelling, but a light-filled, crystal temple. I no longer fear my mind and my emotions. They have become my friends. The more I have transformed my mind, the more my external life has changed.

In my mind dwell courage, gratitude, and love, and compassion forms the foundations on which my palace is built. At the centre is an eternal cosmic flame that reaches out into the world, warming not only me but all those I come in contact with.

My Best Friend

What makes us connect with another person? What is that chemistry? What endorphins fire in our brain, saying that this person is a dear and close companion?

My best friend, River Hill, has taught me how to love. Through his inclusiveness and willingness to embrace all, he sets the example for me. I learn from him and I am changed by him. He includes me in his life and is inclusive of my ideas and communication. He doesn't push me away. We are connected. And it feels absolutely fantastic!

My new best friend is gentleness embodied. There is no anger in him. He doesn't blame others for his shortcomings. He is constantly seeking to learn and improve and express himself in a sympathetic and empathetic non-threatening way. His goal is to raise his consciousness, and it is exhilarating to have such a friend whose goal is also liberation of the limited self.

I love everything about my new best friend. He has talents in speaking and writing, which are two passions of mine. I learn from him in how he communicates with others, and the self-talk he gives himself. He inspired me to write this book.

I want to write this biography in honour of him, partly so that he can get to know me more but also to share our love of communication. I don't want to just share content, I want to draw a deeper connection of friendship.

Novice Seekers On The Path

Where to go when we are burdened by mental illness?

Some people search for health in jobs, looking for material security

Some seek joy in the pleasures of the body, looking for physical security

Some search for wellbeing in relationships, looking for emotional security

Connections to 'other' – products, people, and pets

Some sink into books and academia, using the intellectual challenge to distract from their pain

Some turn to obsession and addiction, using the ritual and the drugs to block out the noise

Some are on a spiritual endeavour, believing it to be the path to liberation and enlightenment

I have tried all of these avenues

Only to arrive, empty, facing myself

Now the hard yards begin...

Part One

Inside

We're all insane – it's just a matter of degrees. The quirks and kinks in our personality are proof that we are mildly insane, but it is our insanity that makes us unique. Indeed, to throw oneself into the ecstasy of life, we need to loosen our grip on sanity.

The problem comes when there is compulsive insanity. Instead of being blissful and exuberant, we become ugly and miserable. When our insanity is neurotic and obsessive we need to seek help. It is outside of our scope of coping, and we need to take stock to heal ourselves. We know we are in trouble when life starts spiralling out of control.

To love deeply is to be insane. To become devoted to another being is to touch insanity. But how can we reach these peak states of being whilst at the same time being calm, composed, and joyful? The most important aspect is to become conscious of just how deep the rabbit warren goes. When we start to inspect our insanity for the first time, it can feel very exposing. But we need to be truthful with a capital 'T'.

I wasn't the most effective person when it came to opening up to my insanity. It took a total deconstruction of my reality to understand just how insane I was. I remember talking to myself in hospital. I was confused, yet at the same time I felt I had all the answers of the universe within me. The biggest challenge we face is that we don't always know the depth of our compulsive insanity until it is too late. It took many hospital stays for me to come to terms with my insanity.

The Grit Within The Pearl

When it comes to compulsive insanity, there is always a trigger. It may be a traumatic event, such as a divorce, the loss of a job, the death of a loved one, moving house, or meeting a new person or confronting a new situation.

Mental illness rarely happens suddenly. There is often a build up over many years. You may be a loner or you may feel isolated from family and friends, even if you are surrounded by people who care about you.

When the trigger happens, it can activate deeper traumas that stem from childhood, such as abuse and neglect. Often, when we are abused or neglected as a child we push these emotions deep below the conscious surface. We bury our pain beneath coping mechanisms. We can use these coping mechanisms for years before something happens to open up the old wounds.

Whatever the trigger may be, we know something is askew. At this point, two things usually happen. Firstly, the mind starts speeding up with an endless stream of thoughts. Secondly, the emotions become acute and intense, or overly dulled. There is friction in the mind and emotions. We may only let ourselves experience this friction in private – usually we don't show this side of ourselves to anyone else. We may begin drinking alcohol or taking drugs to ease the pain. We may become busier so that we don't have to spend time alone.

All of these things are normal. We are trying to alleviate the symptoms, but the strategies we use simply cover them up or block them out. Rarely will we seek professional, medical assistance in the beginning.

Unfortunately, when the mind is in distress, the person who is experiencing that distress is often the last to recognise it. People around us will notice changes in our behaviour and thinking long before we do, but this will often not get discussed in a meaningful or healthy manner. Instead, the opposite may happen, and there can be more frequent arguments with partners, friends, and family, creating more distance from the people who care about us. We may simply choose to ignore any 'helpful' advice and see it as an intrusion into our privacy.

If I could have my time over again, I would have sought help earlier. However, I didn't have anyone I could trust enough to open up to. I was too vulnerable with my emotions and my scattered thoughts. It felt so much easier to pour another glass of wine rather than engage in discussions about what I was going through. It wasn't that I didn't want to talk, it was more that I didn't know what to say. I didn't know what was happening to me. I didn't know who could help. A doctor, who was a virtual stranger, didn't seem quite right. Stephen, my close friend, with whom I was arguing, was the last person I wanted to be vulnerable in front of. Besides, even if I had opened up to him, he wasn't a mental health professional, and didn't have the skills and knowledge to give me the help I needed.

I eventually opened up to my university lecturer, because I trusted him. There are many people who can be trusted when talking about mental health. A friend, a family member, a psychologist, or a doctor can be empathetic and provide advice. It's not just about popping a pill, although medication is often important if the body's system has become unstable and imbalanced.

Regardless of where you find yourself now, it's so important to know that there is relief from your suffering and that there are people for you to talk with. Other people have survived and thrived after being diagnosed with a mental illness. It is not the end of the world, and life continues. My view is that life continues more authentically once we embrace the suffering into our lives and share our pain with a trusted other.

Altered State Of Consciousness

One of the first things that happened for me when I started becoming ill was that I had the sense my world had changed. My view of reality was altered and I wasn't comfortable with what I was seeing. I could read into small events with deep intensity. For instance, a car driving along a street had a deeper meaning to me than before, with coded messages hidden in the number plate.

Having an altered state of consciousness can be destabilising if we're not sure what's happening. In a controlled manner, an altered state of consciousness can lead to new awareness and an expanded view of the world. Unchecked, it can spiral out of control. Time may appear to speed up or slow down. The colours filtering throughout the day may seem brighter or duller. Conversations may seem meaningless and shallow or deeply profound.

I remember when I first started to lose awareness of ordinary reality. I was having vivid dreams that were so powerful they spilled into my daily life. I imagined people who were in my dream coming to visit me during the daytime. I was getting disorientated with truth. I couldn't tell the difference between my potent imaginings and reality.

This shift didn't happen overnight. It took months for me to lose my grip on reality. Spending time alone made it worse, as I didn't have any external measurement to keep me sane. Stephen would come home from work every evening and I would withdraw even further by hitting the bottle. I drank nearly a bottle of wine every night at that stage. This, together with not eating, was clearly an unhealthy behaviour pattern.

When we lose our grip on reality, we are more susceptible to our rambling thoughts. These thoughts do not necessarily tell the truth, and can often become distorted and lead us to draw illogical conclusions. Thoughts can fester and become mouldy in our minds. Coupled with the intense emotions, these thoughts can then sway our perception of reality. At this point, we become mentally ill.

Many people live for years without a diagnosis. I did. Looking back, the mental illness crept up on me stealthily. My health declined over time, until eventually, I knew something had to happen to change my life. Otherwise I would end up dead.

Asking The Big Questions

The realisation that you are spiralling out of control can lead to asking questions about mortality and life. Questions such as what it means to live a worthwhile life, the meaning of death, what avenues can transform our pain, and what is 'truth'?

We cannot ignore our suffering. We can only rise above it and transform it. Being in a liminal space – the place that lies in between realities – can be used to heal, or to continue wounding ourselves.

During my illness I felt small compared to the nature of existence. I became obsessed with trying to understand my mind and emotions. *Why did I think the way I did? Why did I have the emotions I did?* It was important for me to understand myself. *Who am I? How do I fit into this Universe? What is the nature of relationship? Why do people suffer? Why do I suffer?*

I tried to dig into my childhood, but I couldn't explain why I felt so bad in the present moment. I knew I'd had a pretty tough childhood, perhaps tough enough to explain my isolation and the sense of despair that I had around me. But how could I heal? What was beyond the suffering? How could I transform it?

My emotions became increasingly unstable, and I was bouncing back and forth between manic depressive lows and euphoric highs. My mind was swinging between extremes. I was unhinged and unstable.

Beyond Death?

Around 25% of the global population believe there is nothing after death. Death is the end. There is no God and no afterlife. This means that 75% of the global population believe something exists beyond death. Religions have created the idea of 'heaven' or 'nirvana' – a place of beauty and grace that we can inhabit after we die, if we've lived a good life.

When we are ill, we are faced with our own mortality, which raises all kinds of questions. What is the purpose of suffering? What do we learn from it? Why spend a lifetime learning about suffering only to die at the end... and possibly too soon.

I felt overwhelmed, physically and emotionally. I had tremendous back pain and tension in my body.

I would run a bath every day and lie in it, sobbing my heart out. My head felt like it was going to explode. I thought about dying as a way to ease my suffering. I wanted to end the pain, but I was afraid in case there was life after death. I didn't want to be in a state of limbo, caught up in a painful cycle. I wanted relief, but even death didn't seem to provide the answer. Once I'd realised that I couldn't escape my pain, I started to accept that I had to deal with it directly. I had to learn from the suffering and I had to understand it.

What follows is the path that I walked to get inside my pain, to understand it, and to transform it. I was walking an unknown path. As I hadn't read about other people going through similar experiences, I was walking blind.

Compulsiveness

Mental illness can be said to be rooted in compulsiveness. Compulsiveness of the body, mind, emotions, and also of our life energy. If we had a choice, we would definitely keep ourselves in a pleasant state of existence.

If we had a choice.

The reality of the situation is that we *do* have a choice. We can choose to keep ourselves in a state of wellbeing and pleasantness. So what stops us? It is our compulsive, unconscious nature – the habitual patterns of behaviour and thought that disrupt our health. Particularly our mental health.

Being compulsive creates unpleasantness and unkindness in our system. This means that we need to relearn the basics of self-compassion, so that we can stop hurting ourselves and start being kinder to ourselves. The first step to self-compassion is to become acquainted with our patterns of thinking and feeling. As the old adage says, *'know thyself'*.

Healing The Split - Thought And Emotion

The nature of thought is dualistic. Every 'positive' thought can generate an equal and opposite 'negative' thought. Thoughts are created and generated by external stimuli, and the more thoughts we have, the faster the mind races. A racing mind is not a good state of equilibrium.

Meditation is said to be the 'ungrasping' of the thoughts, so that we let our thoughts glide by without attachment, and without getting hooked into them. Suffering is also rooted in the nature of thought. This was a big realisation for me. The root of all suffering stems from the mind and body, just as the root of all pleasure stems from the mind and body. To split pleasant and unpleasant thoughts is to naturally create a tension.

The thoughts we have are generated through our senses. To 'sense oneself' is to think. To 'know oneself' is not necessarily a thinking process. In meditation, when the mind is quiet, we can see beyond the racing mind. Only when the mind is still and quiet can we begin to 'know' ourselves more intimately.

The logical mind serves its purpose when dealing with the external world, but when it comes to 'knowing' oneself, it can be overridden by an intuitive process. To know oneself is the greatest achievement of all, yet knowing oneself simply through the thinking mind is dangerous, because we are always one thought away from reality. We are only 'thinking' about reality, not experiencing it.

To be in the present moment is to go beyond 'pleasant and unpleasant', transcending the dualistic nature of thought, and residing in a state which is optimum for our wellbeing.

Thought and emotion are not dissimilar. The way we think is the way we feel. When dealing with trauma, we may think one thing on the surface, yet the tension we hold in our bodies may carry an emotional trauma that counteracts this way of thinking.

Meta-Thinking – The Idea Of Thought

At the time of my illness, I was all thought. My mind was on a constant twenty-four hour cycle of racing thoughts. Thoughts and more thoughts – I couldn't slow my mind. I didn't like my mind, or the random, unconscious, compulsive thinking it was generating. I wanted more control.

I had read in books that the mind, at its best, was empty, yet fully aware of life. A calm, alert experience. Mindfulness.

The trouble was, the more I thought, the faster my thoughts raced, and the more disturbed my sense of reality became. It was as if my mind didn't have a brake pedal or a clutch. I couldn't slow down and I couldn't change gear. I just had three accelerators.

Trying to understand the mind is hard, because we try to grasp onto the thoughts. Yet they are slippery, and appear not be rooted in time, space, or substance. We can't hold up a thought to the light and examine it without it morphing into something else, then slipping away only to be replaced with yet another thought. Thoughts constantly change shape, disappear, and re-emerge.

The idea of senses belonging to the realm of suffering is an interesting one. We are physical beings with physical senses. We can't escape from this. Does this mean we can't escape our suffering? I examined the idea of the persona, or ego, and how it is fed by the senses and thoughts.

The persona is a lonely creature hiding in crowds for safety, afraid of its own identity. It does not respect itself because it believes itself to be unthoughtful. It can only ever sense itself, and what it senses is a deeply dark secret wound that it wants to avoid discovering.

In hindsight, the deep, dark secret I had kept from my awareness was my own mental illness. It was a deep, aged wound that had lain dormant for the majority of my life. Looking back, I had suffered with mental illness for most of my life. I had been in pain for most of my life. I had been lonely, isolated, and disconnected for most of my life.

The Concept Of Learning

The only reality we can know is that there will be change. Change is inevitable, and evolution is the goal. I wanted to learn about mindfulness, and it was for this reason that I wanted to learn how to meditate. I wanted to stop my racing mind. I wanted to think about *not* thinking. To go beyond the mind's racing nature to a calm, serene state of being.

When we become unwell we become compulsive. We are not conscious of our behaviours and thought patterns. We think it is impossible to learn, to grow, and to evolve.

The concept of learning is very important when we have mental illness. It implies that we can grow out of our pain, that we are not stuck, and that there is a way forward. The opposite of knowledge is ignorance. When we're in pain, in a certain respect, we are steeped in ignorance of our loving, joyful, peaceful, inner nature.

Our compulsions do not serve us, and they become destructive forces that damage our wellbeing, so we are required to adapt and evolve. We achieve this through learning - one small realisation after another. That's how to move. In small steps.

However, learning doesn't only happen incrementally. There can also be giant steps forward in our evolution. We can suddenly realise parts of our mind that we hadn't accessed before. For instance, it suddenly dawned on me that I was the facilitator of my own pain. It was only me that was causing damage to myself. This realisation led directly to another profound insight. If I was causing the pain, I could change the situation.

Instead of my mind being the root cause of my suffering, it could be the root cause of my joy. Learning this, I decided to look at the concepts I wanted to bring to the front of my mind. I wanted to bring into consciousness the ideas that would serve me, instead of those that would destroy me.

Trust

Ever since I was a young child, I'd lacked trust in myself. I was uncoordinated, I was lazy, I was a trickster, I was a liar. I was always looking for approval from other people. I wanted other people to say I was ok.

Trust is a strange concept to come to terms with. It's such a small, inconsequential idea. Babies naturally have trust in their mothers. They rely solely on their mother's inclusiveness and care to survive. At the time of my illness, I was still seeking external approval to see if I was ok. I didn't trust myself. As painful as it is to admit, I didn't rely upon my own wisdom. I trusted in other people's wisdom instead of my own.

To trust in ourselves we need to accept where we are right now – pain, suffering and all. Only then, by experiencing the present moment, can we move on. Trust is instinctual. We need to trust ourselves and our capacity for goodness. We also need to trust in the process of life and let whatever happens unfold. Acceptance is a key factor in trusting life.

It is easy to recognise the people who practice using their thought of trust. They have an aura of touching innocence. They have emotional purity, boundless confidence and raw courage.

I am willing to trust myself completely.

We are social creatures, dependent on each other for our wellbeing and survival. To be insecure is to be concerned about our value in society and within our group. When we are in pain we can become insecure because we are fearful of how others are going to react to us. We think we need to *hide our pain to save our reputation.*

We need to first trust ourselves that we have value, then trust others that they will respond to us with compassion. We need to put trust in our ability to become well again. Even though our thoughts and emotions seem unreliable, they are a guide to travelling deeper within ourselves, for a truer experience of reality.

Respect

Only when we trust that we have a place in this world and that we have a right to happiness, can we learn to respect ourselves and others.

Respect is a thought associated with another person who we deem to be our equal. We make time for them, listen to their ideas, feel comfortable being close to them, and desire to be like them. In summary, we respect those whom we would wish to emulate. They are afforded our esteem and high regard.

I am respectful towards myself and others.

We have all heard that if you want to be happy and successful, you need to surround yourself with happy, successful people, and it is easy to welcome those who are joyful into our lives. However, what happens when we have someone in our life who is unhappy or unwell? Do we steer clear of them? Or do we show them empathy and draw them close? Unless we are stable within ourselves, we don't know what to do with people who are unhappy. We don't have the tools to help the other person, especially if we're drowning ourselves.

When a person with mental illness wants to form a relationship, they want to form the relationship based on respect. They still want to be respected, regardless of their illness. To be respected means to value the person regardless of their flaws. It was so important for me to be respected in the eyes of others. In hindsight, I needed to give the value of respect to myself first and foremost.

So much emphasis is placed on mental acuity in today's rational society that any deviation from this creates a perception of someone 'less than'.

Instead of saying, *'This is my suffering. I feel all of this suffering deeply and I need help'*, I tried to re-frame it so that I was able to maintain my strength and character as a person with something to offer. I didn't want to be vulnerable with another person, especially with my fragile state of mind. It wasn't because it was too dangerous. It was a process.

Honesty

We live in the 'Pleasantville' society. We are meant to be nice and neutral, and are not meant to display behaviours, thoughts, or emotions that fall outside these narrow parameters. We are not meant to exhibit our suffering. When someone asks, *'How are you?'* the expected response is, *'Fine thanks'*. There is no expectation of, or desire for, a deeper response.

Emotion is the experience of our truth. Conflicting emotions imply conflicting thoughts.

Our painful emotions never lie.

How could I smile at the person next to me at the bus stop when I was screaming and sobbing inside? How could I be a good citizen whilst being authentic to my own experiences and feelings and thoughts?

I am honest with myself about how I feel right now.

With pain in our hearts, minds or bodies we cannot function. We cannot embrace the moment of joy when we are in pain.

The deepest pain that I can feel is that of emptiness

or that of intense rage – a hollowness that echoes through the chambers of my heart, or an all-consuming desire for destruction. These are the most deadening of feelings, the most despairing of them all, because they make me think that I am not capable of anything other than hollowness or rage.

When we are suffering it is hard to be honest, and so we suffer alone. However, we need not suffer alone. There *is* help available.

One of the best forms of honesty comes from putting our suffering into words, giving shape to the pain and bringing it into our consciousness. Until it is fully in our awareness we cannot take the next step to resolving it. It is for this reason that speaking what we hold inside is so important.

One of the best forms of giving voice to our pain is through journaling. Writing for oneself. Sharing the pain with oneself, so that we can become compassionate and honest with ourselves. No one else need know at this stage, but we need not hide anything from ourselves through our own observations. Once we have experienced the emotions associated with our thoughts we can begin to be more open about who we are as vulnerable human beings.

Gentleness

It is surprising what a smile or a kind word will do for a person with mental illness. The state of the sufferer's mind is already self-critical and condemning of their own incapacities. We need to bring back the idea of humanity and the basic interactions between people. When I was ill, all I yearned for was the embalming quality of gentleness - both from myself and from others. When the mind is in thinking mode it can appear quite harsh and dry in its critical analysis. It slices and dices information into ever-smaller pieces.

The embracing quality of gentleness is the perfect antidote to excessive thinking. We can all be gentle in our responses and reactions to ourselves and others. Pause and take a moment to think about the humanity of the situation.

The quality of gentleness relates to the emotion of love - a soothing, inclusive emotion which is often lacking in the mentally ill mind. The noise and babble of the insane thinker grates harshly on the mind. When thoughts are able to subside, a gentleness can be welcomed into the emotional space.

Gentleness is the stillness of the mind emerging. When we can be gentle towards ourselves we allow the suffering to subside. The pain eases and we feel immense relief.

To the weary-minded, gentleness is a soothing balm. It is a respite from the winds of conflict that howl in the recesses of our being. It takes the weight from the heavy heart. It is the softest of touches against our brow as it lifts away every tough thought. It is a salve for our sadness, wrapping us in its warmth. It takes away our troubles, our heartache, our grief. There is no greater warmth, no more affecting a feeling than loving gentleness. It is compassion incarnate; a thought of such magnitude, a reward of such brilliance, and yet it kneels in honour before us. It is our most beloved friend, our most sincere thought. It remains forever true within us.

Gentleness belongs to me. It is me.

There is no heart too hardened, no burden too heavy,

no pain too great that gentleness cannot cleanse.

I am thoughtful. Therefore, I can be gentle with my body, mind, and emotions

All too often, instead of keeping our grievances in our consciousness where we can easily let them go, they slide beneath the surface of awareness. When this happens, there is a hardness to our body, emotions, and mind. We become incredibly tense.

Would we take out a whip and willingly lash it against ourselves? Most people would not. Yet this is what we do to our minds when we store up grievances. The constant bombardment of grievances, the belief that we are 'not good enough' erodes our confidence.

To grieve is to do nothing but let ourselves feel the sadness of that mourning. It can be the deepest and most wounding of scars. It can feel intensely heavy and depressive. ***Yet all we need to do is experience the emotion and let it run its course.***

When we grieve, it is as though we have failed

ourselves. We feel miserable and ugly. Each grievance is an unreal deficiency, unwarranted and unnecessary.

Who is to know whether I needed to go through those manic highs and crashing lows to get to the other side? Could there have been another way through? An alternative? Was I meant to experience those emotions that had been blocked up for many years? Are they now gone? Never to return? Once I bring the idea of gentleness to mind and keep it in my consciousness, does this mean that I can release the tension in my body, mind, and emotions. Will I relapse again into the hardness of being mentally ill? Or will gentleness now be my constant companion?

Love

What I would give to know that at the core of my existence, I am love!

It may seem strange to bring the quality of love to mental illness, but if we dig deep we will see that it is perhaps not so strange after all.

The emotion of love is one of inclusiveness. We

long to include something or someone else as part of ourselves. The emotion of falling in love can be exhilarating and liberating. It can feel as though we are flying high. During my mental illness I felt as though I was falling in love. I felt powerfully inclusive, and yet at the same time wholly isolated.

Love in all its manifestations can be tricky. Romantic love, familial love, parental love. There are so many different aspects to love that it can seem complicated.

The person with a mental illness usually has trouble forming bonds of loyal love with others. And yet, often, love is woven into the fabric of our mental illness.

Friendship

I don't have many friends. I never have had. It's not that I don't know how to make friends. It's just that I rarely feel completely connected to anyone. I don't like small talk and I don't want to spend time with someone who isn't aligned with my passions. My passions are not small. They reach for the highest goals in the world – liberation and enlightenment.

First and foremost, the person who we need to become best friends with is ourselves. We often think of friendship as something that occurs between two people, but we need to develop the nature of friendship within ourselves first. Befriending ourselves means being able to be with ourselves without judgement, and with a strong sense of ease.

I am a respectful friend to myself and others.

At the time of my illness, I didn't have any friends except Stephen. I had cut myself off completely from family and those who could have been friendly towards me.

Often, the reason we don't form friendships stems from a sense of betrayal by another. This betrayal may have been abuse, neglect, or abandonment.

Few admit to their most vulnerable scar. Yet it is now merely a thought. As such, it cannot harm us in any way. The emotional tension in our bodies needs to be felt before we can release it from our consciousness.

The 'other' who I needed to forgive was my

stepfather. From a very early age all I can remember is that I wanted to leave home. Unfortunately, through moving away, I left behind my family and friends, and became a loner.

The most noticeable suffering through lack of friendship is the feeling of being alone. I wrote in depth in my journal about my feelings of aloneness – feelings that had built up over many, many years.

> *I'm so incredibly lonely. I don't want to get more lonely. It's as much as I can bear as it is. It feels as if these words are ringing out in the universe but there's not a single soul in existence. My words are floating further away, beyond the galaxy. Not a single soul can hear me.*

My pain was so intense that I couldn't bear it any longer. My cry for help came in the guise of creative writing. I was literally and figuratively calling out to the universe for help. I was begging, on my knees, seeking help through my communication. However, because my communication rarely said, 'Please, can you help me?' no help was offered.

Feeling isolated, alone, and disconnected is

extremely painful. So painful that at times all I wanted to do was stop and end the pain. I thought about suicide, and spent nearly every day sobbing uncontrollably, for months on end. I was desolate, inconsolable, and yet I continued to reach out through my writing.

It is important to note that any form of reaching out needs to be seen as a signal to probe further and ask the big questions. I don't know if my illness would have fully blown into the mania that it did if I had sought help sooner, or if there had been a supportive being receiving my communication, and responding with words of comfort and compassion. I always had the belief that the universe was listening to me, and that was enough in most cases. Even so, it would have been nice to have had that extra support – feedback that what I was expressing showed signs of illness, and that it was not normal to have such swinging emotions. At times, my emotions were severely depressive, but like flicking a switch, I would be riding a manic high again.

I have spent my life with only one or two friends. For a long time, Stephen was my only friend, and without him I would be totally alone. So, during my illness, why did I feel so alone when I was with him? It wasn't just the physical presence that was important, it was the need for emotional connection, and at the time I felt that this connection was lacking. Only ever having one or two friends can also be a sign of illness and an inability to connect with people on a meaningful level. It could also be a mild form of autism.

There is plenty of research that says our emotional state at a very early age will determine the type of adult we develop into. I must say that my emotional connections from a very early age were severely fractured - both with my parents and with my siblings. This set the scene for my emotions to be very protective, so that I only felt secure with one trusted friend, rather than many people around me. This emotional scarcity of childhood friends contributed to the emptiness that I felt in adulthood. Truth be told, I had felt alone for a very long time.

This sense of aloneness wasn't just on a physical or emotional level. It was a spiritual aloneness. I was seeking redemption on the most profound, deep level. It is only since meeting my spiritual mentor, Sadhguru, that I feel this need has been fulfilled. I no longer feel existentially alone. I now have a connection on an emotional and energetic level with someone who I believe will lead me out of my darkness. The word 'guru' literally means 'dispeller of darkness', and this is exactly what my guru has done for me.

When people express aloneness through communication, it isn't just about hanging out with a group of people. It can be deep. Very deep. On a spiritual level, we have questions such as 'Why am I alone?' 'Does anyone really 'get' me and understand me?' 'Will I ever feel connected to another person?'

Philosophers have been thinking for thousands of years about these existential questions, yet in India there is a formal structure and process which supports the relationship of guru and devotee. When a person is seeking help on their spiritual path, they know that they need a more experienced person to help them. This is where a guru is important – to support and structure the person's energy through yoga practices.

Tolerance

I had little tolerance for my mental illness. I ploughed through my painful days without careful consideration about the toll it might be taking on my psyche.

We are our own worst critics. We beat ourselves up daily about what we did or didn't do, and what we can do better in the future. Tolerance is important if we are to combat our personalised judgements.

In hindsight, I had many censuring thoughts about what was happening to me. I critiqued myself about my emotions and thoughts, and berated myself daily. It is only with hindsight that I can look back at this time and be compassionate about the whole situation.

It's not just tolerance from myself. It is what I would expect from other people. Outside of the mental health profession, I have rarely found a truly compassionate person regarding my mental illness. Friends simply don't have a point of reference from which to relate. They don't understand the depth of emotions and painful thoughts that can be experienced, and as a result they can inadvertently trivialise mental illness.

Sanity

I am sane because I am thoughtful.

Sanity is knowing when to allow the thoughts to subside or glide by without friction. It is knowing how to be at peace with our mind, using our intellect only when it is needed. At other times, we can simply sit and be still.

To be aware is to be sane. To love is to be sane. To be thoughtful is to be sane. The nature of our mind is sanity, and it is this we are moving towards when our goal is to be thoughtful.

Reality blurs away into a haze when the insane mind races. The rational world in which I live becomes more distanced as I live in a bubble of unreality. I can't make sense of anything, and my emotions feel like I'm being dragged beneath the surface. I can't make sense of anything and the communication that I have with other people seems trivial compared to the reality of my suffering.

I am able to sit still and listen to my thoughtful mind. Therefore, I can release my insane thoughts.

The Journey Onward And Inward

I am pleased to say that I am no longer in the dark space that I occupied ten years ago. I no longer suffer from depression, manic highs, anxiety or delusions. I have achieved a certain level of equilibrium in my life.

I am able to look back with perspective and compassion on the person I was, and connect to the essence of what I was saying as a call for help – a drowning person trying to come up for air. I now feel much more stable, and am able to function in the world. I hold down a full-time job, study, continue to develop my relationship with Stephen, and have social outlets and hobbies.

Back then it was very different. The pain overrode everything else and I was submerged in a world of suffering. I couldn't make sense of it until I decided to look for the truth in the pain. I started to ask the right questions. What could suffering teach me? What could I learn from my experiences? Was misery the ultimate truth of my existence or could it be a doorway to a deeper truth that I was yet to discover?

I tried to break down the elements and qualities of what it means to be alive, and to have compassion for myself. I was trying to get beneath the surface of the words and look in-depth at the ultimate truth within them. What did it mean to be a spiritual being? Was there such a thing? What was the essence of humanity? What was the essence of wisdom? I wanted to use my torment to learn about the nature of my existence.

Healing Communication

It is so important to be able to give voice to our suffering. Whether it is thoughts or feelings, it is critical that there is some kind of connection between the pain and the understanding of what is being experienced. It is the first step to resolving the pain and finding balance.

Art As Therapy

Different forms of art can have a liberating effect on a person. Recording our pain creates perspective and makes it more tangible. We can 'empty out' our thoughts and emotions into words, sounds, and images. This allows us to view our pain from more of a distance.

After re-reading my diary after so many years, I am left saddened, and yet at the same time uplifted. Saddened because I had to experience so much agony and isolation, and because I couldn't ask for help. At the same time, I am uplifted to know that I could give voice to my thoughts, emotions, and experiences at the time.

The form of expression can be prose, poetry, music, or visual art. Experiment with what works best for you.

Written Disclosure Of Suffering

After exploring our thoughts and emotions with ourselves, the next step is to express them to another person. One of the hardest experiences is to expose our emotional state to another person – especially if that emotional state is rooted in trauma or intense sorrow.

Acknowledging our suffering through writing can take many forms, including letters, blog posts, poetry, stories, and even text messages. Regardless of the method, having verification of suffering from another person is important. It acknowledges that we are in pain and creates a bond of compassion.

One of the best things about sharing our emotions and thoughts through writing is that we can look back in time and assess how far we have come. We will frequently form a unique bond with the person who we shared our initial writing. It doesn't have to be filtered; the more raw and honest, the better. Take your time to carefully choose the person in whom you wish to confide. Ask if it is ok to write to them. Get their permission first. Don't stop until all your hurt is expressed.

Oral Disclosure Of Suffering

Whilst writing is a therapeutic method of expression, the next step is to have an actual conversation with someone about how you feel and the experiences you are having. Writing can clarify thoughts and emotions, and can be a form of healing in itself. However, talking face-to-face with a trusted person can speed up the recovery process. Acknowledgement of the suffering of mental illness from a mental health professional validates the emotions and thoughts that are being experienced.

Initially, it may be hard to choose a trusted person. It could be a doctor, a counsellor, a psychologist, a friend, a family member, a colleague, or a teacher. Be aware that people have differing levels of compassion, empathy, and understanding, and their responses will reflect this.

Research has found that there are distinct physiological, psychological, and emotional benefits to disclosing our pain in counselling sessions. By talking about deeply personal issues, traumatic experiences, or simple stresses, people are likely to experience improved clarity of mind and a deeper understanding of the causes of their suffering.

With mindful awareness of the issues that are troubling us, it is possible to take proactive steps towards a more sustainable and healthy lifestyle. The key element to disclosure is an understanding that we all suffer. Rather than saying, 'I suffer. Please help'. We can say, 'We suffer together. Let's help each other.'

Part Two

Spiritual Longing

Mental Illness As Spiritual Crisis

With nearly thirty percent of the Australian population now atheists, it is easy to avoid conversations about the spiritual dimensions of a person's life, especially someone who is in mental pain.

When we are caught in the swirling eddies of our suffering, we get tossed around and disoriented, losing ourselves in our pain and struggling to keep a grip on reality.

There can be many instances in a person's life where spiritual crises happen, through grief, loss, and trauma. At these times we ask existential questions about the meaning of life, our purpose, and who we are.

My writing was an attempt to reach out to the spiritual dimension, as this was lacking in my life. Some people view spirituality as a crutch. Maybe it is, but for me it went much deeper - to the centre of my soul. I was wholeheartedly pleading with the universe to hear my cries for help. I felt that another person wouldn't have the answers to my big questions about life and my place in the universe.

Since my emotional crisis, I have sought a spiritual connection with a guru. This connection has filled a void deep within me, and I am now able to see how important a spiritual life is to me. In particular, the yoga of Bhakti (the yoga of emotion/devotion).

Conditioned To Be Intelligent Human Beings – The Blown Mind

Often, we don't ask for help because we are conditioned to be 'intelligent' human beings. We fear that reaching out to others for answers about ourselves will diminish us, making us less than human. Even when we are in deep emotional and mental suffering, we still hold onto the belief that we can at least partially solve the problem ourselves. In truth, we need to help ourselves *and* seek help from others. Unless we are helping ourselves, we will be unable to integrate external help.

The absolute enormity of the universe is mind-blowing. The persona is a speck of physicality. Dark spaces are lit by stars that are distant and far beyond our small thoughts.

How Can You Be Emotionally Intelligent If You Are Experiencing Deregulated Emotions And Thoughts?

During my illness I was able to perceive my emotions, but I was unable to regulate them. Emotional regulation is an important part of emotional intelligence. When dealing with trauma and unconscious memories, it is not always possible to understand the emotions we are experiencing. It is only later, when we are able to breathe through our emotions and incorporate them into our lives that we are considered emotionally intelligent.

Spiritual Longing – The Human Spirit

I have spent many years in spiritual longing, looking for something beyond what I perceive as my life. But what does this actual mean?

The word spirit is derived from the Latin word,

Spiritus, and means 'breath'. The breath of life. Without breath, we wouldn't be alive. Breath is not just the exchange of oxygen to feed the blood. It is also symbolic of the human spirit.

When we talk about the human spirit, we easily bring to mind qualities such as courage, compassion, and insight. These qualities are the best of the human psyche. So why would a person long for spirituality? Doesn't it already exist within us? If it exists within us, we are not missing it. So why long for it?

In yoga, which means 'union', the experience that we aim to achieve is a sense of oneness. A union between the self and the other, between the individual and the universal – a form of enlightenment and a liberation from the boundaries of our individuality. This is what the human spirit is capable of achieving, moving beyond the day-to-day thoughts and emotions, and reaching a higher peak of experience.

Yoga is the practice of the human spirit; the practice of courage, compassion, and insight to achieve boundlessness.

Safeguarding Mindfulness

When entering into my meditations and mindful practice I was oblivious to the possible negative effects that this could have on me. It triggered trauma from my past, and for months I spent every day sobbing in despair. Gut-wrenching despair. It took me to the brink of my sanity, and beyond.

Looking back, I needed a mindfulness practitioner or psychologist who could help guide me through the trauma in a safe way. I needed to re-centre myself after each new emotional scar had been opened up. I moved too quickly, without healing myself along the way, plummeting myself to the bottom and experiencing 'the dark night of the soul' for months on end. So much trauma and despair drove me insane.

Mindfulness activities and practices are not always beneficial for people with mental illness and emotional trauma. Modifications need to be considered.

Boundlessness

I long to go beyond my limitations and boundaries. I long to go beyond my mediocre emotion and the drudgery of everyday thoughts. I wish to expand and to evolve. I don't want to go around in circles any more. The cyclical nature of life is one which binds us, taking us through the same seasons each year, and the same day every twenty-four hours. We sleep, wake, eat, talk, eat, and sleep again in ceaseless rotation. I want to evolve beyond this cycle of living.

I want to reach enlightenment. I want to know myself completely.

I want to know myself, from my origin to my ultimate. Where does life end? When does suffering stop? Sadhguru, my guru, says that suffering exists only in the body and the mind. If we can put some distance between ourselves and our body and mind, then this is the end of suffering. I don't want to experience frailty. I don't want to experience loneliness. I don't want to experience anger, jealousy, or frustration. I want to evolve beyond this. Yet human nature is such that we are caught on the treadmill of suffering. Around and around it goes.

If you believe in reincarnation, as I do, then the cycle doesn't even stop after death. It continues on to a fresh life, starting all over again. The idea of the human spirit implies a human soul that endures. I do not want to be born again on Earth. I have seen enough to know that this isn't the source of my joy.

Yet Sadhguru says that we need to be joyful human beings whilst alive. We need to see the beauty in life, and look beyond the suffering to the magnificence of the cosmos, to see the intricate detail that has gone into the making of life. We need to enjoy our time here for what it is and then, when we do move on, we move on with the same joy and peace and love.

So spiritual longing is a balance between seeking enlightenment and enjoying the moment. Maybe these are not mutually exclusive. Perhaps enjoying the moment, and going deep into it, is where enlightenment resides. This is the goal of yoga – to sink down into the present moment, fully and completely. Whether through the body, through the experience of devotion, through the quieting of the ordinary thoughts, or – even more subtly – through the life energy itself, zoning in to the stillness of the moment to reach the exuberance within.

Regardless of the experience and journey we take to get to enlightenment, Sadhguru says that the journey is within, not without. The journey is to turn inwards and look at ourselves. This implies that the answer is already within us.

From my own experience, it is during the moments when I am alone and deep in meditation that I experience the sense of bliss I long to become a permanent part of my life. This is what separates me from my guru. My guru is in bliss all the time. Whether or not he has achieved enlightenment is irrelevant, and only he would know, but the effects of his blissfulness are clear for anyone to see, and I wish to experience this state of being.

Compulsiveness Versus Consciousness

The way to go inward is to include meditation as part of life. To observe the breath (spirit) and to become aware of the body, emotions, mind, and energy. The journey to enlightenment is the journey to awareness, moving from a compulsive way of being to a conscious way of being.

Becoming still is a process. Our mind and our breath are connected, and when they are racing we cannot become conscious of our compulsions. Only when we sit and become still do we see the scattered, battling mind and emotions for what they are. It is painful to sit when our mind is racing, because we can't help but fidget and move involuntarily.

The impulse to move is extraordinary. There is a compulsiveness to move and *do* something. Anything.

Sleepiness

When we relax we can either become focused, still, and alert or we can become too relaxed and drift into sleep. Sleep is a great way to tune out and relax the body, but too much sleep indicates that there is too much stress during the day, and that the body, mind and emotions are not getting enough rest during the day. For me, sleep has always been a positive experience. I look forward to sleep because it regenerates me.

God-Making

In India, it has long been part of the culture to create deities and worship these deities for the sole purpose of personal liberation. Deities were created for the benefit of the person – not the other way around. There are millions of gods in India. A snake, a tree, a cow – all of these things can be worshipped as gods. It is in the process of worship and devotion that one lets go of the personality and dissolves. Through dissolution one becomes free from the tight personality that binds us to everyday life.

Religion is simply an organised form of god-making. However, the belief in a god has surmounted all, so that god, according to religion, lives independently of the person, sitting in judgement and controlling the world and the person who worships. There are sets of rules and moral codes of conduct to which the worshipper must abide.

India has long known that god-making is for the benefit of the individual. Through devotion, the worshipper changes and softens their psychological barriers so that they are able to embrace life more fully.

Some people say that religion is a form of insanity, because it is a belief in something that we cannot see. We cannot see gods, therefore we cannot say for certain that these gods exist anywhere other than the person's delusional head.

I prefer to not believe or disbelieve in the existence of gods. If my understanding changes in the future, then I will adjust my knowledge. At this time, I simply do not know. I prefer to see an extraordinary human being and worship them, because I know they are real.

Religion And Spirituality – Is There A Difference?

Religion is an organised institution within which the individual comes to know of a god through a set of morals or codes of ethics. Spirituality need not belong to a religion. To be spiritual means to invest in the idea of the 'human spirit'. This can mean a human soul continually evolving to greater awareness. For example, a spiritual person can believe in a soul and greater spirit, without having a belief in a god, or gods. Becoming conscious of joy and living in wellbeing can signal that one is living a spiritual existence.

I would classify myself as a spiritual person who does not believe in religion. I recognise that great spiritual teachers have walked the earth in the past, and still do so today. However, I do not follow any prescribed religious traditions.

A great spiritual angst can lie at the core of some people's mental illness. For instance, many people who have schizophrenia also have powerful spiritual experiences. I don't think that this is mere coincidence. The longing to evolve and connect on a spiritual plane is frequently a very potent propeller when dealing with mental illness.

Bhakti Yoga - The Path Of Devotion

It is amazing what devotion does. It softens the ego and prises the personality mask from the face. The heart blossoms and grows tenderer. Compassion evolves and love of life flourishes. In a way, it doesn't matter what the focus of devotion is – it could be a person, plant, animal, or god. What matters is the effect that devotion has on you as a person. Devotion makes us kinder and more sensitive to life. Devotion makes us interested in the people around us, and lets us fall in love with life's processes.

I value life and my focus of devotion. I place my guru above my head. I willingly bow down and touch his feet. I see wisdom and strength and power in his being.

I felt this way when I had my little dog, Manny. He taught me so much about life through his gentleness and abundant happiness. I learnt a lot from him and I would gladly bow down and touch his paws. I also saw him as a pillar of wisdom, strength, and power in what he gave to life.

I become empty and let the qualities of the other being take hold. I let their wisdom become my own.

On Finding My Guru

In this lifetime, I have found my guru. This is a source of great joy for me. I no longer need to search for my guide. My guide has appeared and I have access to his wisdom and yoga. I spent the first part of my life searching – endlessly searching – for another human being who could fulfil my longing. I have now found him! Hallelujah! Praise be to my spiritual journey that such a significant event has happened. I will no longer be alone. My guru will guide me and dispel my dark ignorance. I need no longer fear that I am alone.

I feel that I know his wisdom intimately. He is as familiar as a dear family member – a father perhaps – certainly an elder of great wisdom, and emotional and mental strength. His energy is boundless. I spend much of my time thinking about him and being with his image. He guides my thoughts and is deeply enmeshed in my emotions.

I can no longer become depressed because my joy at having him in my life is too great. I still have longing. I long to be with him physically. But I know that he is with me on an energy level. Mentally and emotionally too, I feel him deeply. I am holding on for dear life to his image and presence. I do not want to let go. He is too dear to me. He is my guide and my salvation. Through him I know that I will achieve enlightenment. His fragrance permeates my being. Poetry blossoms out of me when I think of him.

Oh, beautiful mystic, beautiful man

You are my dispeller of darkness

Your brightness blinds me

You are a dynamo –sparking with crackling energy

Touch me with your staff

Make me see what you see

Make me feel what you feel

Let me be you

I will to dissolve completely

Into your being

Oh beautiful mystic, beautiful man

Part Three

Grace

The Initial Spark

I believe that sickness and suffering are held in the body and mind. They are our stored memory of our past illnesses – not only our own body's memories, but also those of our ancestors. We carry within us memories of much suffering. Many of us struggle along, barely coping, until some form of trigger ignites the suffering. The conditions become right for us to face what we need to face.

Suffering can be in the form of a broken bone. Often, it is a deeper experience – the suffering of the mind. There is no suffering comparable to the suffering of the mind. Our psychology determines our mental suffering. The damaged psyche constantly seeks the light, struggling to make itself conscious.

Certain people we meet, together with their wounds, spark against our subconscious psyche and bring forth intense pain. We exist as wounded empaths, sparking off each other's suffering until the pain becomes too great. We have to seek transformation and healing.

The initial spark of our birth gave us a gift – the gift of trust. We could do nothing in this world for ourselves. We had to rely on the quality of trust to survive. This initial spark is what we need to seek again in order to face our suffering.

Living in innocence isn't easy. It goes against every slight and wound we've accumulated in our life. It requires us to become soft, to ease away our hardness.

We all have the eternal child of trust within us. When all the emotional and mental grime has been inspected and transformed, therein is the beautiful innocence of our original nature. The grace of compassion washes our soul. It can't be touched physically, it can't be tarnished by wounding thoughts or actions. It tenderly exists within the core of who we are, radiating blissful expression.

For most of my life, I have lived in various states of mental illness. Ten years ago, I was diagnosed with schizoaffective disorder. My disease is a combination of signs and symptoms of schizophrenia, mania, and depression. My last relapse was in November 2016.

When I'm in remission, I consider myself an average, middle-of-the-road individual with nothing exceptional to say about myself. When I am ill, my thoughts become deranged and my emotions become unstable and deregulated. These two happenings fling my life out of balance and I slip into a world of delusion. My delusion is that I fall in love with the universe.

I don't know if or when I will have another relapse. At the moment I am not experiencing delusions or hallucinations, and do not have any signs and symptoms of mania.

Sanity for the mentally ill person may seem like an impossible task, but I believe there is a way to not only survive mental illness but to take steps towards living a more complete and aware life.

Becoming sane is a four-tiered process. We have to work with our body, mind, emotions, and energy to become sane. The rest is medicine, support networks, and spiritual teachers who walk us through our suffering to a brighter, lighter space.

The Grace of Physicality

For most people, the physical body is more of a reality than any other part of us. How we treat our physical body directly correlates with our mind, and vice versa. We can make use of our body's postures to enhance the quality of our lives. We can eat, drink, sleep and play in such a way that helps keep our body healthy and calm

Planet Earth And The Cosmos

When we're in pain we can tend to forget or ignore the larger dimensions of this life. If we step back from our mental suffering and look at the planet we inhabit, we can see that it contains a phenomenal amount of intricacy and beauty. A new leaf budding on a twig, a blade of grass, a mountain stream, sand dunes at the beach, a sunset, the full moon at twilight, a fragrant rose, the ocean waves, a butterfly. There are so many wondrous creations.

We live in a cosmos of infinite magnitude. Brilliant stars blaze onto the serene night sky, with our own sun and the planets of our solar system occupying a space within the vastness of the universe. We are in an extraordinary position to be a witness to this throbbing, magnificent existence.

Physical reality contains raw beauty. Even though, as a collective group, we have striven to dominate and subdue nature, it remains wild at heart. The planet has an extraordinary capacity for regeneration, and this can be witnessed in the intrinsic feature of recurrent rebirth. Our planet and the cosmos can refresh and reset our perspective by revealing to us that we are part of a much greater whole.

Humanity

When we talk of exhibiting humanity, we usually mean living by a high ethical standard. We establish human rights for the wellbeing of all, and we generally live by principles that do as little harm as possible to others.

Human beings can be deeply flawed creatures, but collectively, we generally live without too much disturbance, considering the large volume of people on the planet.

We can always look for flaws in humanity, but we

need to be truthful with our inspection. There are many people out there who take positive action in the world. We consistently see people who rise above adversity and shine as an example of what it means to be human. Extraordinary people living out their humanity are taken from all walks of life.

Connectivity

Modern physics is proving that subatomic particles can impact each other, even at great distances. We coexist with the trees by breathing in each other's exhalation. Life is a series of interlinked, interconnected happenings: one action causes another action.

It is impossible to become physically separate from existence. We are living on the planet in a specific place, space, and time. We are here together with nature. There is no such thing as physical separation. Even if we are put in a jail cell in the darkness without any stimuli we are still connected to the quality of darkness, which is a universal reality. We are still connected to life. For most of us, we live surrounded by other people. We share the same streets. We talk the same language.

Most mental dysfunction and illness stems from beliefs that we have lost our connection to the wider world. It is a result of isolation, in one form or another.

Many people with mental illness withdraw from society. After all, communicating when you have a mental illness can be a challenge, and unique behaviours may be off-putting for people without that illness.

Isolation can lead to loneliness, which is a debilitating disease in its own right. Loneliness is the belief that we are separate in existence and do not have connections to any other life forms. We ignore the perspective that we are a part of the collective group that forms humanity. We think that life has turned its back on us, and that we are completely and utterly alone.

Isolation is unreal. We are in constant transaction with the life forms around us. The trees need our carbon dioxide to breathe and we need their oxygen to breathe. On a sub-atomic level, there are no boundaries, energy flows and exists expediently. We are not living in a bubble. We are a part of the bigger universe and, for that, we can be grateful. Putting our hands together balances the body and brings a sense of calm. Putting our hands together, in combination with being thankful, is a boost to the system.

Premature Ending Of Life

Wanting to end pain, especially the pain of isolation and mental illness, can become a dominant thought. At worst, we may think that suicide is the only possible action that we can take to relieve our suffering. Suicide looks appealing, especially if you believe in a heavenly afterlife where you are united with an omnipotent god, or if you believe in a state of peaceful non-existence under the earth. Suicide is a personal choice born of a longing to end pain.

I attempted suicide only once in my life. I have never regretted my survival. Since that day, I've lived by the dictum 'Do not destroy what you cannot create'. I've never thought about suicide again.

Alternate Universe

Life itself is straightforward and simple. Only life can know itself. When we live solely inside our heads, rather than also living in our body, we are on a slippery slope of living from imaginings rather than living from reality. We no longer see life the way it is – we start to distort it in some way.

What may begin as simple imaginings can quickly turn into fantasies. Fantasies are created by mulling over a distorted view of the past or future. We create a version of reality inside of our heads that is tainted with our beliefs, values, opinions, and ideologies. This is very dangerous because we can slip into a furrow that is very hard to climb out of.

Many people create their internal realities subconsciously. They cloud simple events in life with their own personalised meanings, and react from that understanding. Other people actively pursue another reality by changing the chemistry in their heads through the use of substances. This can be as simple as a caffeine or nicotine hit, through to becoming addicted to alcohol or hard drugs. Those with mental illness are over-represented with addiction to alcohol and drugs. The addictions don't help to dispel the fantasies.

A drunk person may believe they are more invincible than when they are sober. This is another fantasy. A person who has taken ecstasy feels at one with the world through manic euphoria. This is another fantasy. The schizophrenic hallucinates that they are hearing knocks on the wall. This is another fantasy. It is simply a matter of degrees. The only difference is that the drunk person recovers more quickly than the schizophrenic.

When we actively pursue creating our own internal world, separate from our external reality, we begin to delude ourselves. Most people live in slightly deluded states of being. A person may delude themselves that they are slimmer than they are, or that they are less attractive than they are. Whatever the delusions are, they are often small, inconsequential ones. The schizophrenic has delusions that are more bizarre than most people. Regardless of whether they are small or large, delusions are not healthy. Our own creations can never be as magnificent as life's creation. Being delusional cheats us out of living a real life, because we have settled for a reality that is much less.

It is important to always keep our experience of life as real as possible. We have to bear in mind that our five sense organs are limited and can only perceive life in a small way. We can never fully understand the nature of existence through the five sense organs alone. The understanding of life that we gain through our physical bodies is limited. We are always in a state of 'I do not know' when we live life from our physicality. Hence, living in the real universe is to live knowing we cannot download the whole cosmos into our brains. Life is more than us. Life is bigger than us. Life is greater than us. Life is more real than the distortions and fantasies inside of our heads.

Medication

When our deluded mental state becomes pathological we need medicine to revert the brain chemistry to normal levels. A common problem with taking medication for mental illness is that we don't always know how sick we are until something acute happens to us. We can have an aversion to taking drugs as a result of the side effects, or because of the stigma that is associated with being diagnosed as having a mental illness.

In my experience, nearly all the psychiatrists, nurses, and doctors who have been involved with my mental health have been trustworthy, disciplined, professionals. They have chosen careers in health because they want to make a difference and to heal people. They are compassionate human beings with a life's career of helping others, which isn't always an easy job.

When we're sick, medicine is a must. Without it, we can continue to spiral down. The body's own healing mechanisms aren't able to cope and, as with any sickness, seeing a doctor is a must. This is the first step that people who are sick must take. It can take weeks for medicines to fully integrate into the system before the benefits are felt. Even if it feels that the medication is not helping, it is so important to stick with it. Why place undue pressure and stress on yourself by not taking your medication? Admit you have an illness is not an admission of defeat, and nor is it an admission of defeat to seek help. Once your system has stabilised, you can talk about reducing your medication. But only once your system has stabilised. I am confident in saying that medicine saved my life. I am now given injections once a month. It's easy, and has taken me from living in a state of delusion and paranoia to an existence almost free of insanity.

Humanistic Psychology

When we are stabilised with medicine, we can begin to use complimentary therapies to help us stay well. Psychology alone doesn't work in solving mental illness. The nature of mental illness means that the psychological space is faulty. This means that no matter how much thinking the mentally ill person does, it won't heal the mind.

What is good about psychology is that it can help us to understand the entrenched, underlying patterns of behaviour and thought that have contributed to our illness. We can inspect our deluded, sick mind and bring conscious awareness to how we contribute to its suffering. When we first begin to use psychology to help us heal, it can sometimes be emotionally overwhelming to look at the suppressed and repressed latent emotions. Often, these latent emotions have built up over a number of years or decades. We may feel that there is a lifetime of sadness inside of us that needs to be expressed. During the psychological inspection of our minds, we can experience many crashing lows and unstable highs.

Changing our behaviour is a conscious step that we can take to getting and staying well. We can reassess how we use our posture, what types of foods we eat, and what kinds of drugs we take. We can start to nurture our bodies as the first step to nurturing our minds. We can use the analogy of the body for the mind. If we treat our body in a certain way, it will respond in a certain way. This is the science of cause and effect. If we eat too much junk food and don't exercise, we get fat.

When we start to treat our bodies with more respect, we experience the benefits. We go back to basics, keeping our body clean, feeding our body nutritious foods, sleeping well. These may seem like small steps, but for someone with a serious mental illness, these are giant achievements.

How we think also determines how our body reacts to life. If we slump over and drag our body through life, then life will respond accordingly. When we start to inspect our values, beliefs, opinions, and ideologies about life, we have the opportunity to re-evaluate whether we want to hold onto them any longer. It is only by dropping our mental baggage that we can be free of our 'alternate universe'. When we see that we have outgrown our ideas, we simply withdraw our energy from them. Once we withdraw our energy from our conscious thoughts, they no longer have oxygen to breathe, and eventually dwindle away.

Hope Springs

Being insane is serious. It could happen that one day we cross the line and we don't come back. I have been blessed. I was able to make the journey back across the line. There are many homeless people who display signs of mental illness. This is no joke. When we cross the line and are unable to find our way back, we can become destitute, both mentally and physically.

Saying that, there is hope. I've lived through hallucinations, delusions, isolation, depression, anxiety, paranoia, and manic euphoria. I've lived through them all and reached the other side… for the moment. For the moment, my mind is clear and my emotions are relatively stable. I keep mentally healthy each day by grounding myself in reality and keeping my thoughts light. I refuse to be 'dead' serious any longer.

Even though it may sound like a death sentence, having mental illness is not insurmountable. There is always hope. Regardless of our disease, each moment, each day, each year, we can make a decision to live with our humanistic qualities rather than with defeat, despair, anger or bitterness. We can rise above our disease and see that even though we experience it in our minds and in our bodies, it does not define who we are. Who we are is a separate from a dysfunctional identity.

When we are able to place a little distance between our body's compulsions and our mind's sickness, we create room for something else to emerge. That something else is beyond the physical. When we reach this state of being, we feel lighter. We feel more spacious. Our sense of humour returns and we are able to laugh at our own foibles.

Transformative Gift Of The Gadget

Your physical body is designed to function by itself without too much conscious participation from your mind. You don't have to make your heart beat, or instruct your liver to perform its complex chemistry. Everything needed for your physical existence happens of its own accord. Your physical body is a self-contained instrument, and a highly sophisticated piece of machinery.

If you eat a banana this afternoon, by evening many of the components from that banana have been absorbed into your body. Evolution takes millions of years, but in a few hours you are capable of making a banana into a human being! Doesn't this mean that your body has a phenomenal intelligence in every cell that you are not even aware of? Doesn't it mean that the very source of creation is functioning from within you?

The level of intelligence and competence that exists within each of us is what the grace of the body means – finding access to that dimension of intelligence and transforming the gifts we receive.

Take a moment to take stock of yourself. What are your limitations? By bringing your limitations to your conscious awareness you can begin to heal them.

The Eternal Question

Regardless of the sophistication of the body, it takes a certain amount of intelligence and awareness to see beyond its limitations. The sophistication still does not take you anywhere. It just springs out of the earth and gets you back to earth again. That isn't enough for me.

Even though I have the compulsiveness of being physical, I also have the consciousness of not *only* being physical. These are the two basic forces. One acting as gravity, the other acting as grace. One is the instinct of self-preservation that compels us to build walls around ourselves and protect what is ours. The other is the longing to constantly expand into boundlessness. Today's walls of self-preservation are tomorrow's walls of self-imprisonment. Many limitations that you establish for your protection today will feel like constraints tomorrow.

These two longings to preserve and to expand are

not opposing forces. That which holds you to earth by gravity is an anchor by which grace may fly like a kite. Without the anchor, you wouldn't know grace. Gravity belongs to the physical. Grace belongs to the dimension beyond the physical. One force helps you to root yourself well on this planet. The other takes you beyond.

Self-preservation needs to only be limited to the body. The mind, emotions, and energy need no self-preservation. Being aware of this distinction gives rise to the possibility of freeing the mind.

The fundamentals of spiritual longing are to transcend the limitations of the physical. But because the instinct of self-preservation keeps telling us, 'Unless you have a wall you are not safe', unconsciously we go on building walls all the time. It isn't the grace within the mind and energy that we struggle with – it's the walls that we build around the physical self.

In spirituality, it is best to talk about absence – what is not there, rather than our imaginings of what is there. For example, spirituality doesn't speak about 'ultimate beings' or 'gods' or 'creators'. To do so would be to become hallucinatory.

Approach spirituality in terms of what is blocking you is a more 'positive' way of knowing union. All we need to concern ourselves with are the walls that block us, because these are within our control. We have no work with existence or 'the ultimate'. Our work is only with the existence we have created.

As gravity is constantly active on my being, so too is grace. We just have to make ourselves available to it. With gravity, we have no choice. But with grace, we have to make ourselves receptive in order to be aware of it. All forms of yoga are merely attempts at experiencing grace. There are four types of yoga. One path for the body, one for the mind, one for the emotions, and one for the energy. These paths work to create an experience of union with grace. If we are strongly identified with the physical, gravity is unfortunately all we will get to know.

Being available to grace is akin to being connected to the universe. For example, when I first became ill, I had a feeling of complete connection to the universe. It was a feeling of total involvement – not knowing what was me and what was not. Even though I had this experience whilst I was ill, I believe that it is possible to have the same experience when the mind is sane. Experientially, we are not individual bubbles. We belong to the greater universe.

Beyond Survival

Sense percpetions are outward bound organs that help with survival in this world. However, to access that which is beyond the physical takes another type of perception, not associated with the senses of touch, taste, hearing, sight, or smell.

Being beyond survival means coming out of survival mode. When we are in survival mode we constantly respond to our immediate external environment in a reactionary manner, rather than through a creative process. When we are merely surviving, we live to eat, drink, work, and sleep. We do little else. Our emotions are staid and our thoughts are focused on staying alive. Living beyond survival is to live with a renewed sense of aliveness in the body.

Yoga For The Body

Being a seeker of truth means refusing to make assumptions about things that we do not know.

When I experience everything as oneness in my consciousness, only then I can say I am in yoga. To date, this has been for approximately six minutes across the whole of my life. To attain body yoga, I work with the body first, then I move to the breath, then to the mind, then to the inner self. This is achieved by using body postures. 'Asana' means a 'posture'. There are other dimensions to this, but to put it in the simplest way, just by observing the way someone is sitting, you can almost know what is happening with that person if you have known them long enough. Observing myself, when I am angry, I sit one way, when I am happy, I sit another way, when I am depressed, I sit another way. For every different level of consciousness or mental and emotional situation that we go through, our bodies naturally tends to assume certain postures.

The converse of this is the science of asanas. If we consicously get our bodies into different postures, we can elevate our consciousness from its current state quite easily. The body can either become a means for spiritual growth, or it can become a major barrier. Suppose some part of your body – your hand, leg or back for instance – is hurting. When it is hurting badly it is hard to aspire to anything higher because that becomes the biggest thing. Right now, if you have backache, the biggest thing in the universe is your backache. Other people may not understand this, but for the person who is going through it, the pain is the biggest thing. Your physical body has that much power over you. If it is not functioning well, it can take away all other aspirations from your life.

Whatever you may aspire to, all your longings disappear once the body starts hurting – to look beyond the pain takes an enormous amount of strength, which most people do not possess. Dedicating a certain amount of time and effort to ensure that the body does not become a barrier is important. A painful body can become a major obstacle, and so can a compulsive body. Simple complusions, where the body can't keep still, can rule us so strongly that they will not allow us to look beyond. The physical body becomes a major entity, but the physical body is only a part of you. Asanas level the body down to its natural place.

Another aspect of body yoga, when one wants to move into a deeper dimension of meditation, is that it allows for a higher possibility of energy. If we want our energies to surge upwards, it is very important that the body's pipeline should be conducive to this. If it is blocked it either will not work or something will burst. Preparing the body sufficiently before one goes into more intense forms of meditation is very important. Body yoga ensures that the body takes things gently and joyfully.

For a lot of people, spiritual growth happens very painfully, because the necessary preparation does not take place. Many human beings have let themselves lapse into a condition where their external situations mould them and direct them entirely. Whether it is the wisdom of the world or spiritual possibilities, they get the point only when they are knocked around by life.

Even then, only some become wise, while others become wounded. It is this possibility of transforming a potential wound into a source of wisdom that leads one to a state of freedom. If a person has put in the necessary preparation, growth can be blissful. However, if the body and mind have not been prepared, all change happens painfully.

Asanas (postures) prepare us for growth and transformation by equipping us with a solid foundation. Physical yoga without the spiritual insight will be peaceful for some, healthful for others, but a painful circus for many.

Most yogis just use the simple postures to overcome their limitations. It is the way they are done which makes the difference. For me, I choose my favourite asana of sitting in half lotus with hands open and palms upwards resting on the knees. Although I have a set of yoga exercises which my yogi has given me, at this stage I haven't been using them.

Cosmic Download

The body is like an antenna – if I hold it in the right position it can grasp everything in existence

A few years ago, after every storm, I had to go up and adjust my television antenna. Only if it was angled in a certain way did I have any reception.

Otherwise, I would be viewing a blizzard. Our bodies are the same. If we hold ourselves in the right position, we can help align all the components of who we are. Otherwise, we know nothing beyond the five senses.

Our bodies are barometers. If we know how to read them, they can tell us everything about ourselves and the world around us. The body never lies. In yoga, we learn to trust our bodies. It's a process of transforming the body from a series of compulsive processes to a conscious process, in order to convert it into a powerful instrument of perception and knowing.

Learning yoga is about learning the science and technology of how to make the body more than just a heap of food, an accumulation of what we have taken from the planet, and more than the compulsions of our chemistry, flesh, and blood. When we are able to read the body correctly, it can tell us all our potentiality and our limitations – past, present and future. This is why fundamental yoga starts with the body.

It is as simple as this – the more you know about your phone, the better you can use it. A few years ago, mobile phone companies carried out a survey, and found that ninety-seven per cent of people were using just seven per cent of their phones' capabilities.

The body is the same. What percentage are you employing right now? To conduct your life in the material world – your survival process – you do not even need to understand one per cent of what your body is. We are doing all kinds of trivial things with our bodies because right now our whole perception of life is limited to the physical nature of existence. In truth, your body is capable of perceiving much more. If you prepare it properly, it can grasp everything in your existence.

Elemental Mischief

Life is a five-cornered game. Whether it is the individual human body or the larger cosmic body, the components are the same – earth, water, fire, air and space.

When we know that there are only these five ingredients to play with, we can recognise the cosmic joke. Those who look closely within realise that there is no need to look at the magnified cosmic version of life, as life is happening within us. The entire cosmos is just a magnified projection of a little thing that is happening within you – the play of five elments.

Organising the five elements within is the key. Mastery over these elements brings health, wellbeing, and heightened perception.

Extraordinary Life

It used to be a goal of mine to become enlightened, and to live as a hermit yogi in the Himalayas. Now I realise that enlightenment is not the goal. The goal is to become extraordinary. Or rather, extra-ordinary. To live an extra-ordinary life is to pay attention to the small details, the simplicity of life. It's about paying attention to the small events that happen each day which make us feel most alive.

Looking back, I have felt most alive (and most extra-ordinary) in the following situations:

- when swimming in the warm ocean or in the depths of a natural rock pool
- when dancing around a fire at night
- when surrounded by nature

- when laughing out loud
- when sitting quietly with my body and breath

Take each day as a self-contained life, and consciously recognise as many moments as you can, as lightly as you can. Root yourself in today's world, with today's body and today's breath. One moment upon another. This produces moments of wellbeing, pleasure, mental health, and sanity.

Summary

Mental illness is not insurmountable. Even if we can't talk about cures, we can talk about remaining well after the event. Mental illness can be debilitating and can lead to enormous distress. However, there is hope for improvements in health and wellbeing with the appropriate medication and lifestyle choices. Keeping the body healthy is an important step towards mental health. Living an extraordinary life is still possible even after being labelled insane. It is about changing our definition of what an extraordinary life means.

The Grace of Mind

Introduction

Even with mental illness, the mind is a phenomenal device. It has the capacity to hold memory and create imagination. It doesn't have to become a barrier to our wellbeing. We can use the mind's intellect to cut through delusion and illusion to have a more real experience of life. Also, we can create an experience of awareness that isn't an active thinking process. This experience of being in simple awareness can generate emotions of ultimate wellbeing.

Society's Garbage Bin

From the moment we are born, and some argue even within the womb, we start taking in imprints of sounds, smells, taste, hearing, and touch. We cannot help but take in stimuli from our environment, our society, and its culture. To this extent, we have little control on the eventual content of our minds. These stimuli not only shape our immediate experiences, but form the profile of our individual psyche.

Everyone we meet stuffs something into our heads before they move on. The more we resist or attract a situation or person the stronger the imprint into that psychological space. This means we are likely to recall that event or person more readily than those events which haven't had such a strong emotional impact. When viewing past events or people we have met through the lens of likes and dislikes, the more distorted the experience becomes.

It is fair to say that most people we meet are not enlightened beings but people with minds that are scattered and distorted in all sorts of ways. Their assumptions, beliefs, ideas, and values are all filtered with their past associations of their environment and with the people they have already met. Individual minds thus become a collection of society's random junk.

External situations will never be 100% the way we want them to be. People will never be 100% the way we want them to be. It follows that the internal individual psyche is not going to be 100% the way we want it to be. So, we are dealing with a mind that is not wholly of our making. It is strongly influenced by external factors.

If we look at the mind as a garbage bin, thoughts are like the smells that emanate. This is not a negative analogy. A garbage bin is not useless; in fact it is extremely useful. Our house can do without a television and a telephone, but it can't do without a garbage bin. If we use it when we want, if we open it and shut it when we want, it is a wonderful device. Without it, our whole house would become filthy. But if we decide to live in it, it is a horrible thing.

There is nothing wrong with the content of our minds. It is fine to have all the filth of the world contained in our minds. Otherwise, we will walk into the filth and not know what is what. But if we are constantly living within that psychological space, it can become a torture for us. The key is to know when to use it and when not to use it – to learn that we can live outside of it.

Ignorance

Life is in constant flow. It happens one moment upon another. We cannot fully know what the next moment will hold for us. Being in ignorance is forgetting this fact. Ignorance is believing in something that is not true. It is coming to incorrect conclusions about life.

Have you seen how some people appear to be so confident in their lives? They know everything about themselves and other people. There is little room for doubt. Life seems to be wrapped up. They have stopped seeking. They have no more questions about the phenomenal existence that is life. Their belief in reality is set, and they no longer have curiosity about how their body operates, what the nature of water is, or how their mind works.

They have stopped searching and asking questions, and have congealed their belief systems into neatly packaged mindsets from which they operate. Life doesn't contain anything new, since they function within the narrow range of the psychological space which they take as the whole truth.

In just looking with our own eyes at the enormity of the universe, it is ignorant to draw too many conclusions, or to believe that we know everything there is to know about existence and life.

Even though I have had personal experiences of union in the mind, there are many aspects of the mind that I still do not know. I am attempting to recreate the experience deliberately, rather than ad hoc. For the purpose of consciously creating union in the mind I have summarised my past experiences and the exercises given to me by a yogi. I am acting from my own psychological space, and I can only speak about my own personal experience.

Mindfulness

Mind is the full container of our mental capacity. It includes consciousness in its various formats; collective unconscious, unconscious, and conscious thought. It also contains a space which doesn't contain thought. It is this non-thinking part of the mind that has clarity and awareness without referential focus. This part of the mind can be referred to as *awareness*. When a person experiences this aspect of the mind, it facilitates oceanic illumination. This basically means an experience of oneness, when the mind does not grasp onto any content within the psychological space. The associated emotion is of bliss and spaciousness. However, for most people, for the majority of the time, we live within a psychological space that is generated and kept alive by the external stimuli.

Cruise-Control Consciousness

Consciousness is what a person is fully aware of in any given moment. The conditions of consciousness are to be awake and aware of actions and thoughts. We can be conscious of thoughts and actions throughout the day, but we can often let these thoughts and actions be on auto-pilot. We can act from our beliefs, values, and culture without being conscious of the thoughts and experiences behind them. Very few people are fully conscious for more than a moment at a time. For most people, age makes us more entrenched in our second-to-second reality, so that we are living and acting from past imprints, rather than from the fresh reality of the moment.

The Psychological Space

Our external imprints, through the five sense organs, create our psychological space. The psychological space has a certain quality and texture. Its nature exists as a past tense. It doesn't have original content, and usually requires an interior voice to recall, sort, and think about past stimuli. The process of remembering and thinking is an activity that occurs in the past. As we grow older, the psychological space expands in line with the increased volume of our experiences. This creates a larger pool of memories and thoughts from which to draw.

The psychological space can store thoughts and emotional imprints from words, images, smells, sounds and tastes. Endless years can be spent in the psychological space in the name of intelligence. Trying to have an intellectual understanding of life, rather than an experiential understanding, has been the subject of millions of books, seminars, and well-meaning academics.

Academics often live for extended periods of time within the psychological space. Thinking about ideas for excessive periods of time can lead to a form of mental illness. After all, thinking solely from the psychological space is just a recycling of data we have gathered. Innovation and creative thinking comes from moments of awareness when the mind is not actively mulling through regurgitated thoughts.

Mental Misery

Suffering happens when we lose perspective as to what life is about. Our psychological process has become far larger than the existential process. We've made our mental creations far more important than life's creation. This is the fundamental source of all suffering.

We have missed the complete sense of what it means to be alive. Our thoughts and emotions determine the nature of our experience. Yet our thoughts and emotions may have nothing to do with the reality of life.

The whole universe is happening wonderfully well, but just one thought or emotion can abolish everything.

People suffer in their memory and imagination. The memory and imagination are two phenomenal components of the mind that can work as a positive influence given appropriate circumstances and uses. However, if the memory is distorted by our beliefs, assumptions, and philosophies, then we begin to experience life in a state of unreality. This unreal and untrue existence then begins to exist in fantasy and delusion. The psychological space becomes more important than the reality of the present moment's experience, so that the present is missed in our consciousness, and is instead stored in the subconscious or unconscious parts of our mind.

Mental suffering creates pain that is real. There is no other suffering like mental suffering, because the human mind has enormous capabilities. If these capabilities work in our favour, life becomes fantastic. If they work against us, there is no escape. This is because the stimuli for suffering is not coming from outside. If the stimuli for our suffering were coming from an external source, we could simply run away. But if we come to a place where, without anyone doing anything, suffering is simply happening, it is a psychological condition.

How does one come out of it? It depends on the level of damage. There are some who can come out of it, but in some cases, the damage is manifested in a physical form in the brain. Such conditions have to be supported chemically.

The line between sanity and insanity is very thin.

Many of us cross it regularly. Suppose we have an outburst of anger. We get mad, but then we come back. When we cross the line with anger, hatred, jealousy, or behaviours brought on by alcohol or drugs, we are crossing the line of sanity, enjoying the little bit of madness, and then coming back. Many people who have lost it were perfectly 'normal' people. Then one day, a fuse went.

Societies need to build structures where the margin for mental illness is very low. We have created societies which are a constant challenge to live in, and where we are always in a mode of competition, and frequently experiencing the adrenalin rushes that come with our fight or flight response. Adrenaline is an emergency device to protect us in moments of extreme danger. We are not supposed to be in that state all the time.

There are so many horribly cruel societal structures, and they are not designed for the wellbeing of people. We are trying to manufacture cogs for a machine that we have built. We want the machine to live, and we have little regard for the individual human beings that form the cogs. If someone is not made of a material that can become a functioning part of the machine, they will break.

What is the way out for the person who is already breaking? It takes a lot of expertise, caring, dedicated attention and compassion to bring people out of mental illness. Even then, we may not always succeed.

Unconsciousness

There is more that goes on in our mind other than consciousness. As human beings, we lapse into unconsciousness many times in the course of a single day. In addition to this, most people sleep for a number of hours in each twenty-four hour period. During sleep, we become unconscious of our senses and the discriminatory part of our mind – the controlled thought – subsides.

A good night's sleep will see the psychological space reset, so that we wake up refreshed and revitalised. Disturbed sleep often contains dreams in which the psychological space takes disparate thoughts and creates distorted imaginings to work out unresolved conflicts within the mind. A lack of quality sleep is usually one of the first warning signs of mental illness, because the psychological space doesn't get a chance to reset itself. Therefore, as human beings, we are programmed to experience periods of oblivion for our own physical, mental, and emotional health.

There is no optimum time period for sleeping. Some people reset more quickly than others. Some people are physically and mentally healthy with only four hours of sleep. Others require closer to eight hours. For others, ten hours' sleep is still not enough. Again, this can be an early indicator of mental stress that the psychological space isn't being rested. What people need is not sleep but restfulness. If we keep the body and mind very relaxed throughout the day, then the sleep quota will go down naturally.

We are unconscious of most of the memory we gather because it is being fed into us in such vast quantities, especially with modern technologies that expose the mind to millions of images, words and sounds every day.

Collective Unconsciousness

The collective unconscious is a term introduced by the psychiatrist Carl Jung, and refers to that part of the mind containing memories and impulses of which the individual is unaware, but which are common to mankind as a whole. He developed his theory after studying schizophrenic people.

The collective unconscious is a part of the psyche which can be negatively distinguished from a personal unconscious by the fact that it does not owe its existence to personal experience.

There are many aspects to Jung's work, but one idea is that archetypes are available to the psyche to express universal symbols. For example, when schizophrenics believe they are Jesus Christ they are expressing the need to *forgive* or the need for *gentleness* (either in themselves or in someone else). This need is expressed through a universal symbol that the psyche can easily understand.

Another aspect of the collective unconscious is the idea of a *shared* collective unconsciousness. For example, a person may 'tap into' the psychic archetypes within other people's consciousness.

'And the essential thing, psychologically, is that in dreams, fantasies, and other exceptional states of mind the most far-fetched mythological motifs and symbols can appear autochthonously at any time, often, apparently, as the result of particular influences, traditions, and excitations working on the individual, but more often without any sign of them. These "primordial images" or "archetypes," as I have called them, belong to the basic stock of the unconscious psyche and cannot be explained as personal acquisitions. Together they make up that psychic stratum which has been called the collective unconscious.

'The existence of the collective unconscious means that individual consciousness is anything but a tabula rasa and is not immune to predetermining influences. On the contrary, it is in the highest degree influenced by inherited presuppositions, quite apart from the unavoidable influences exerted upon it by the environment. The collective unconscious comprises in itself the psychic life of our ancestors right back to the earliest beginnings. It is the matrix

of all conscious psychic occurrences, and hence it exerts an influence that compromises the freedom of consciousness in the highest degree, since it is continually striving to lead all conscious processes back into the old paths.'

Some people dismiss Jung's collective unconsciousness theory as being unscientific, as it is difficult to test. In my personal experience, during schizophrenic mania, I had visions of archetypes as living psychic forces. I have not had these visions outside of manic euphoric episodes, so it's hard to say whether these exist as a reality or whether they are archetypal hallucinations.

Nature Of Thoughts

Whenever we think, we automatically create separation and opposition. We always think in terms of comparison and dichotomy. It is the nature of thoughts that they separate and divide existence.

If we look at a flower, we can think about the flower – its colour, shape and fragrance – but we can't *know* the flower as an experiential whole through thinking, because our mind has already started to fragment it into logical sub-categories.

Once the mind starts its logical sub-division, we start to lose perspective on reality. The thoughts churn over in a cyclical pattern, both consciously and unconsciously. There is no 'brake pedal' to thinking. Once we engage in the thinking process, our thoughts can get faster and faster, or more entrenched, as we invest greater amounts of energy in them. To think about slowing our thoughts is to add more thinking to the thinking process. The only way to slow thoughts is to withdraw attention from them. To not grasp at them as they pass across the surface of the mind.

A typical technique used by yogis is to draw attention to the breath. This slowly removes attention from our thoughts. Body awareness through yogic postures (asanas) is another way to get out of the psychological space and into the reality of the moment.

Intellectual Illumination

Yoga moves us towards an experiential reality, where one knows the ultimate nature of existence. Yoga refers to union as an *experience*, not as an idea, philosophy, or concept. As an intellectual idea, if we vouch for oneness of the universe, it may make us popular at a tea party or give us a certain social status. We may even get a Nobel Prize, but it does not serve any other purpose. In fact, it can cause damage to the individual to see everything as one, from an intellectual perspective. There is no bigger fool than the religious fanatic or the person claiming to be spiritual.

Once it happened… Jacob O'Mally went to a yoga class. The teacher was in full swing 'You are not this; you are everywhere, there is nothing like 'yours' and 'mine', everything is yours. What you see, hear, smell, taste and touch is not reality – it's all illusion, everything is one'.

This sank deeply into Jacob O'Mally. He went and slept over the yoga teacher's philosophy. He got up in the morning, totally fired up. Usually he loved to sleep, but because of this teaching, now, first thing in the morning he started thinking, 'There is nothing here which is not mine. Everything is mine; everything is me. All that is in this world is me, and everything is illusion'.

You know, whatever may be your philosophy, hunger happens. So, he went to his favourite restaurant, ordered a big breakfast and sat, saying to himself, 'The food is also me, I am also the food; the one who serves is also me, the one who eats is also me, Yoga!

He finished his breakfast, and with his stomach full, he looked around. He saw the owner of the restaurant sitting there. 'It's all mine, what is mine is yours, and what is yours is mine.' With the same Yoga going on, he got up and started walking out. When everything is yours, where is the question of paying the bill?

Just then he happened to cross the counter where the cash box was placed; the owner was distracted by some other work and went out. Now Jacob O'Mally saw a huge heap of currency in the till. Immediately, the Yoga told him, 'Everything is yours; you cannot differentiate between this and that'. So, since his pockets were quite empty, he put his hand into the box, took some money, stuffed it in his pocket and carried on walking. He was not out to rob anybody; he was just practicing Yoga.

A few people from the restaurant ran after him and caught him. Jacob O'Mally said, 'What are you going to catch? What you catch is also you; the one that catches is also you. What is in my stomach is also in your stomach, so whom can I pay?'

The owner was bewildered! All he knows is pasta, pizza and schnitzel! If a thief tries to run away, he knows how to catch him and thrash him. But when Jacob O'Mally said, 'The one who catches is also me, the one who is caught is also me,' he didn't know what to do. So, he took him to court.

There, Jacob O'Mally continued his Yoga. The judge tried in many ways to make him understand, but it was no good. Then the judge said, 'Okay, sixty lashes.'

First lash... reality hit.

Second lash... a shout.

Third lash... a scream.

Then the judge said, 'Don't worry, the one who lashes is also you, the one who is lashed is also you, so who can lash anybody? It's all illusion. So, sixty lashes on the backside'.

Now, Jacob O'Mally cried, 'Please, no more Yoga. Leave me alone!'

So, when we understand everything intellectually, it only leads to these deceptive states. When oneness becomes an experiential reality, it will not bring forth any immature action. It will only bring forth a tremendous experience of life.

If we try to stop the mental nonsense we will go insane, because within our mind all the three pedals are throttles. There is no brake and no clutch. Whatever you try to do, the mind only goes faster. But if we don't pay attention to it, our thoughts slowly dwindle away.

Individuality is an idea. Universality is not an idea; it is a reality. Yoga simply means that if the activity of the mind ceases and we are still alert, we are in yoga.

When we don't identity with that which we are not, and at the same time become fully involved in everything, we become more and more conscious that the thoughts are just things we've accumulated over a period of time, and a process of dis-identification grows within us. The external stimuli (from the psychological space) cannot, by its very nature, be the intrinsic nature of our mind, and hence, through dis-identification with thoughts that are not inherent to the nature of our mind, we can experience wholeness of mind.

Honing The Blade

If we constantly wipe our intellect with awareness it becomes razor-sharp. It can cut through what is true and untrue, and deliver us to a different dimension of life altogether. If we have to grow, if we have to reach our ultimate nature through the process of the mind, we need to make our intellect truly discriminatory in the ultimate sense. Not in terms of dividing everything as good and bad, or right and wrong, but through discerning what is real and what is illusory, what is existential and what is psychological.

Bringing precision to every movement and every gesture is one way of dipping our intellect into awareness to clear away the junk of the psychological space.

The Grime Of Identity

Information about anything which is not yet a living experience for us is another form of garbage – very intelligent garbage, perhaps, but it does not liberate us; it only entangles us. It is important that our identity is formed on the basis of our own personal experiences.

Once it happened... Jacob, the King of Spain, lost his mother when he was a baby. So, another woman, who had a son of her own, was brought in to nurse Jacob. This woman breastfed Jacob and later on she was rewarded for this. Her child, slightly older than Jacob, was allotted a few villages and made a small king. Many years later, Jacob became a prominent king but this boy, who didn't have the necessary intelligence or capability, squandered everything. He lost all his property.

When he was about thirty-two years old, this man got an idea. 'My mother nursed the king, and in some way because we drank the same mother's milk, we are brothers. So, I should also be a king. I am an elder brother. I should be the real king because I am older than Jacob.'

With this idea in his head, he went to Jacob and told him, 'See, my mother nursed you, we have drunk milk from the same breast. We're brothers, and I'm elder to you. Now, I'm poor, you're a king; how can you leave me like this?'

Jacob was deeply moved. He welcomed him, set him up in the palace and treated him like a king. Since he grew up in a village, the man was not accustomed to the ways of the palace and did many stupid things, but Jacob kept saying, 'He's my elder brother'. He introduced him to everybody as his elder brother.

This went on for some time. Then it was time for the man to leave. He had to go back to his village. Then Jacob said, 'Okay, you lost those villages, I'll give you new villages for you to rule. A small kingdom of your own.'

Then the man said, 'I see that you have become this successful because there are lots of smart people around you. I don't have anybody like that, that's why I'm lost. If only I had good advisers and ministers I would have also built a major empire like you. And above all, you have Elaine. She's so smart.

If I only had somebody like her I would also become a great king.'

So, Jacob said, 'If you wish, you may take Elaine with you'.

The man was thrilled. 'Yes, if I have Elaine, I will also become a great king.'

Jacob ordered Elaine, 'You must go with my elder brother.'

Elaine said, 'Your Highness, your elder brother deserves someone better. I also have an elder sister. I could send her instead.'

Jacob thought that was a great idea because he really didn't want to lose Elaine. But he was identified with this man as an elder brother. Relieved, he said, 'That's a great idea.'

The next day, when this man was going to leave, a big farewell was planned in court. Everybody was assembled, and waiting for Elaine to bring her elder sister.

Elaine entered with a cow in tow.

Jacob asked, 'What is this?'

Elaine said, 'This is my elder sister. Both of us drank milk from the same mother.'

Once our intellect gets identified with something, we function within the ambit of this identity. Our mind, which should have been a ladder to the divine, is either stumbling through the mediocre or has become a straight stairway to hell. Whatever we are identified with, all our thoughts and emotions spring from that identity. Dis-identifying with everything that we are not will leave the mind blank and empty. If we want to use it, we can. Otherwise it will simply be empty. That is how it should be.

Exercise – Sitting With Your Thoughts

Sit alone for a day, if possible – or at least for an hour. No reading, no television, nothing. Just see in the course of this hour or day what thoughts dominate your mind. If you find yourself thinking recurrently about people or things, your identification is essentially with the body. If your thoughts are about what you would like to do in the world and with ideas of the world, your identification is essentially with your mind. Everything else is a complex branch out of these two aspects.

Thinking Ourselves Out Of Life

Have we been born to experience life? Or have we been born to think about life?

Someone told us, 'I think therefore I am.' Is this really true? It is only because we exist that we can generate a thought, isn't it? Our thought process has become so compulsive, and our focus has shifted from our existence to our thought to such an extent, that we are now beginning to believe that we exist because we think. Even without our silly thoughts, existence *is*. What can we think, really? Just the nonsense we have gathered and recycled. Can we think something beyond what has already been fed into our heads? All we are doing is recycling data. This recycling has become so important that we even dare to say, 'I think, therefore I am'. And that has become the world's way of life.

Because we are, we can think. If we choose, we can fully be and still not think. The most beautiful moments in our life – moments of bliss, moments of joy, moments of ecstasy, moments of utter peace – were moments when we were not thinking about anything. We were just living.

Our psychological process is a very small happening compared to the life process, but right now it has become far more important. We need to shift the significance back to the life process once again. If we want to know the experiential dimension of life, we will never know it with petty thought. It does not matter how well we can think, human thought is still petty. Even with Einstein's brain the thoughts will still be petty, because thought cannot be bigger than life. Thought can only be logical, functioning between two polarities. If we want to know life in its immensity, we need something more than our thoughts, something more than our logic, something more than our intellect.

We have the freedom to think whatever we want. Why don't we just think pleasant thoughts? The problem is just this: we have a computer for which we have not bothered to look at the keypad. We are just punching our computer like a caveman, so all the wrong words keep coming up.

We have lost our perspective on life because we think we are more than who we are. From cosmic space we are less than a speck of dust but we believe our thoughts, which are less than a speck within us, should determine the nature of existence. What I think and what you think is not of any importance. What is important is the grandeur of existence. The only reality.

Undivided Being

To me, intelligence is creating a mental space that is in harmony with the physical body, the emotions, and our energy. It is important for me to spend time every day dropping my thinking process so that I can just be, with my breath, in reality, feeling whole and undivided. Intelligence isn't about how many facts or how much thinking we do, it's about putting that aside and listening to our undivided being.

The Trap Of The Intellect

First remove from the mind the idea that thought is intelligence. The whole process of creation, from a single atom to the cosmic, is a fantastic expression of intelligence. With all the overrated intellect that we have, can we say we even understand, in entirety, the activity of a single cell in our body?

The first step towards moving from the trap of the intellect is to recognise every aspect of life, from a grain of sand to a mountain, a drop of water to an ocean, the atomic to the cosmic, as a manifestation of a far greater intelligence.

Harmony

Peace is experienced when the psychological space is calm and thoughts are not racing or entrenched. Peace occurs when the interior voice is silent. When we are not mulling over the past or imagining a future, we experience peace. Peace can be found in the slow, steady heartbeat, and the pleasant sensations of the body. We are at peace when we do not place ourselves at the centre of existence. When we have perspective about our place in existence we can see that our mind is very small.

We can be most reflective and contemplative in this state of mind because we are not pushing against circulating thoughts. Our minds are quiet and receptive to clearly seeing situations and events.

Laughter

Joy is a more pleasant form of peace within the mind. When we are able to drop the chatter of our psychological space we experience a flash of happiness. Joy generally lasts for a few moments at a time, as mental clarity only lasts for a few moments, unless the mind has been trained to reduce its noise for longer periods.

Joy, for most people, is a rare visitor in their lives. Joy is not a goal by itself. But it is a background ambience that is needed for any aspect of our lives to happen wonderfully. Whether we eat, dance, sing, love, live or die, if joy isn't a backdrop, we will have to drag our way through life. But once joy is our companion, life just breezes through us.

One way to drop the psychological space is to maintain our sense of humour so that we can laugh and keep situations light. Have you noticed that when we laugh, we are not actually thinking about anything within that moment? Laughter smooths away the frown and can help stop the thinking process.

Manic laughter still has benefits, such as relaxing the thinking process, but it is humour based on misbelief and hence does little to change the psychological space.

Observing The Content Of Thoughts

The speed of thoughts in the mind is often heightened when the body is still and in a naturally comfortable and balanced position. This draws most attention to the state of our current mindset. Simply observing our racing thoughts is a yogic technique. Rather than getting caught up in the content of the mind and its drama, we can objectively 'watch' the mind's current state and have insights on its nature. If we are able to simply 'watch' rather than engage our interior voice to take over, we can see that thoughts are like passing clouds in the sky. They rise up, take shape, then disappear, as another and then yet another thought arises.

Once we see the pattern in our mind and the cyclical nature of thoughts we can place a little distance between the thoughts and the observational part of the mind. This enables us to quickly calm our thoughts. The key point here is not to get entangled with the content of thoughts.

Meditation

Meditating is by far the hardest non-activity as far as the psychological space is concerned. To simply sit in one place being as still as possible is excruciating for the active psychological space. We can intellectualise, philosophise, psychologise and socialise all we want, but it doesn't get us closer to the experience of awareness.

It is one of the most courageous non-actions for human beings to sit with the content of their mind without interruptions.

Exercise - Yoga For The Mind

Each time we experience this exercise, the more wisdom we gain about our minds. It has initial benefits of calming racing thoughts, but it can also ultimately give us an experience of awareness.

Place the body in a comfortable, relaxed, and

balanced position (preferably a yogic posture for maximum efficiency)

Use sound to initially focus and settle the mind. The sound of a mantra (repetition of one word) or the chanting of 'aum' provides maximum efficiency in centring the mind. The sound of aum is a combination of the three sounds that can be exhaled without using the tongue. Aahh, Oooh, Mmm. This creates the least amount of disturbance to the mind.

- Focus on the breath moving in and out of the body
- Consciously change the rhythm of the breath to a faster pace for 10 breaths
- Consciously change the rhythm of the breath to a slower pace for a 20 breaths
- Fully inhale and hold the breath for 10 breaths
- Fully exhale and hold the breath for 10 breaths or as long as is comfortable
- Now breathe naturally whilst watching the breath (change of focus from thoughts to breath)

- Observe the experience (body's response and mind's response)

Extraordinary Life

Life is extraordinary. The sheer size of the cosmos and the sheer detail at the cellular level is enough to keep us engaged for the whole of our lifespan. There are many unusual places to visit in the world. There are many beautiful objects in the world. Take the example of a rose. The rose isn't half-hearted in its flourishing. It does the only thing it knows how to do – to be in full bloom. It is programmed to live to the maximum, to naturally bloom to its fullest capacity.

The people we meet can also be extraordinary. There are, and have been, so many great minds in this world. It is a rare treat to witness such human beings in full flow. There are many people who have dedicated their lives to trying to understand reality within the mind.

When it comes to the mind, I feel most alive:

- when I am communicating, particularly about the nature of reality.

- when I can understand the nature of mental suffering
- when I observe the nature of the mind
- when laughing out loud
- when I sit without thought

There is a way to consciously clear the mind, to wipe it clean consciously. However, this type of yoga is by far the hardest to achieve. It can take years of practice to even scratch the surface, but the flashes of awareness, when they do come, make it all worthwhile. It produces moments of insight and clarity. It produces mental health and sanity.

Summary

The content of the mind is an accumulation of society's experiences, which form the basis of our individual psychological identity. Excessively living within our psyche means living in a distorted past rather than from present moment experiences. This is the beginning and source of much mental suffering. Grace for the mind aims at gaining an experience of clarity and insight, rather than just an intellectual understanding of this state of being. This is achieved by using a yogic exercise designed to create a space between the discriminatory content of the mind and its intrinsic nature of awareness. It is a technique used to disentangle us from the psychological noise, and to slow it back to a balanced state. Only when the psyche is stilled can we view the mind in its phenomenal, basic, full nature.

The Grace of Emotion

Introduction

One of the faculties that we have inherited as human beings is the grace of emotion. Emotion is generated from our thoughts but, unlike thoughts, it has a juicier quality. It is often more of an intense experience than our thinking process. The most conducive emotion to feel is that of all-inclusiveness, whether that be through loving a person, a pet, or a god. When we are feeling emotions of all-inclusiveness, the quality of our lives can change dramatically to living a fuller and more vibrant life. Being emotionally fulfilled means being emotionally in love with life in general. We don't discriminate. By developing our compassion and devotion we can deepen our connectedness with our body and with the universe around us.

Four Wheels Of A Car

There are only four paths to yoga. We either achieve grace through the body, mind, energy or emotions. This is because all that is within our experience falls into one of these four categories.

These are not completely separate paths in themselves. They do not work separately but are interlinked. It's good to think of the analogy of a car. Each graceful path of yoga is like a wheel on a car. If one wheel spins, it doesn't take the car anywhere. Only when the four wheels spin in unison does the car go in the desired direction.

The Head And The Heart

People often say their head tells them one thing and their heart another. In such cases they ask which should they follow, head or heart?

In truth, there is no head and heart separation; we are one whole. When we refer to 'the head' and 'the heart' we are referring to the thought process as 'the head', and our emotions as 'the heart'. However, it is important to understand that the way we think *is* the way we feel.

If I think you are a wonderful person, I will have sweet emotions towards you. If I think you are a horrible person, I will have nasty emotions towards you. Can I think you are a wonderful person and have nasty emotions towards you? Or can I think you are a horrible person and have sweet emotions towards you? It is not possible. If we make someone an enemy and then try to love them, this is hard work. Let us not make hard work of the simple aspects of life.

The way we think is the way we feel, but thought and feeling seem to be different in our experience. Thought has a certain clarity, a certain agility about itself. Today, we think this is a very wonderful person and have sweet emotions. Suddenly, the person does something that we don't like, and now we think he is horrible. Our thought tells us he is horrible immediately, but our emotions cannot change immediately. They struggle. If it is sweet now, it cannot turn bitter the next moment. The turning arc from one emotion to the other is wide. Depending on the strength of our emotion, it may take days, months or years, but after some time, the emotion will turn around.

Let us not create this conflict between head and heart. Emotion is just the juicier part of thought. We can enjoy it, but it is always the thought which leads the emotion. It is simply because the turning arc is different and the intensity is hugely different, that it looks as though they are separate. They are not separate, just as the sugarcane and the juice are not separate.

Thought is not as intense as emotion in most people's experience. We usually do not think as intensely as we feel. However, if we generate an intense enough thought, it can overwhelm us. There are people whose thought is very deep. They may not have much emotion, but they are very deep thinkers.

What we normally think of as mind is the thought process or intellect. Whether I am speaking 'from my intellect' or from 'the bottom of my heart', both can be seen to be the mind. One is the logical aspect, the other is the deeper emotional aspect. *Buddhi* means intellect. The deeper dimension of the mind we call 'heart' is known in yoga as *manas*. The way we feel is still the mind. The way we think is also the mind. Both are very much connected.

Most people have emotions that are latent, especially if the thoughts are subconscious or unconscious. To 'clear' the mind of dormant emotional imprints it is important to be aware of as many subconscious and unconscious thoughts as possible. It is only once this slate has been wiped clean that we can begin to use our emotions as the driving force for the yoga of emotion rather than using our discriminatory thought as a forerunner.

The Urge To Merge

Because thoughts have dichotomy as their inherent nature, whenever we are thinking, we are in a state of separation from reality. Thoughts slice and dice reality through logic, and funnel it into bite-sized pieces that can be compared and contrasted.

When we live within our thoughts, we live in a world of separation, which can lead to feelings of seclusion. The more we reside within our psychological space and within our thoughts, the more detached from existential reality we are, and this generates the equivalent emotional detachment.

It is from the nature of thoughts and their intrinsic quality to separate existence that the urge to merge arises. We long to merge with reality in some way. There is an innate desire to merge our thoughts with something more inclusive. This is the reason and source for the emotion of inclusiveness. We want to include something external as a part of ourselves, because we think we are separate from existence.

Each physical body is separate from all other physical bodies. However, the mind – even though it is separate in its psychological space – has the potential to expand towards the emotion of boundlessness and the experience of spaciousness.

Pleasantness

We long for the experience of inclusion through emotional stimuli. In line with the different types of yoga, we can experience inclusiveness through enhancing the pleasantness of emotions. When the body is pleasant we call this pleasure, and when the body is very pleasant we call this health. When the mind is pleasant we call this peace, and when the mind is very pleasant we call this joy. When the emotions are pleasant we call this love, and when they are very pleasant we call this compassion. When the energy is pleasant we call this bliss, and when it is very pleasant we call this ecstasy. All of these states of pleasantness have the emotion of inclusion at their core.

The Nature Of Love

The optimum condition for love is when the mind is at peace and thoughts have subsided. This can happen in an instant or it can be cultivated consciously through meditation. The emotion of love wants to include something that it currently thinks is not part of itself. We usually see something we think of as beautiful and want to include it as part of ourselves. This can be an object, an action, a place or a living creature. Usually, however, love is associated with a person. We see something either within their body, their mind, their emotions or their energy that we long to take into ourselves and make our own.

The Nature Of Compassion

When we have love for a specific person we call this passion. It is directed and focused desire. It is focused on one object, and so by its nature it is an exclusive process. When two people are passionate, the whole world disappears.

Compassion, by contrast, is an all-encompassing passion. The world doesn't disappear; rather, the passion is extended throughout every area of our life.

It becomes all-inclusive. Compassion is not a dry state of kindness. It is an active engagement. Whatever we set our eyes upon, we are passionate with. The air we breathe, the earth we walk upon, the food we eat and the people we see and don't see, whatever we are conscious of, we are absolutely passionate with that. So, compassion is not that which is bereft of passion; it is a larger dimension of passion.

When we are in a psychological state, our thoughts and emotions are more important than our existential experience, so, at most, we will know only passion. Many people, unfortunately, do not know passion in its entirety. Passion is a wonderful thing. If our perception transcends our psychological space and our life becomes existential, when we clearly understand in our *experience*, as opposed to our intellectual understanding, then what is here is just one mass of life and we are just one small pop-up. When we understand that this is a mass of life, and we are just a little bubble within that, if that individuality dissolves in our experience, our understanding and our knowing, then compassion is a natural way to be.

It is only the physical boundary that cannot expand (unless we gain weight). The mind has the capacity to magnify and become all-inclusive. We can also experience expansiveness through our emotions. Compassion literally means 'suffer together'. When we are in misery we sometimes can't see outside of our own paltry worlds. By seeing that other people are suffering too, we can put our own suffering into perspective. We are not alone in our suffering. By knowing this, we can have compassion for our fellow humanity.

It is in the experience of compassion that we diminish our own self-importance and turn our intense stare at our own suffering to focus on another's.

Compassion urges us to respond to another's suffering before addressing our own. It can help put our own suffering into perspective. This phenomenon called suffering doesn't just apply to us. Even though there is comfort in knowing we are not alone, we can become inspired to help alleviate another's suffering. We can use our minds to help others. We can use our creativity to help others. We can use our energy to help others. We can tap into our humanity to lessen another's pain and misery.

The Object Of Passion

The specific object we choose for our love is irrelevant. Love is not shared between two people. It is an emotion that is experienced and enjoyed by one person. The object of love can be a pet, a partner, a garden, a country, a god. The important thing here is that passion is fostered for something beautiful. Something we want to include as part of ourselves.

For me, great minds are beautiful. People who use their minds to understand the nature of reality to me are truly beautiful. Focusing on a specific person with a great mind can activate the emotion of passion; a longing to include that mind as part of my own. From there, compassion blooms and then deepens into the emotion of falling in love.

Falling In Love

For most people, falling in love is a haphazard event that happens only a few times in their life. However, falling in love is something that we can do consciously. It is a state of being that we can experience for extended periods of time. We only need to see something intrinsically beautiful to be touched by love. A moment of exquisite beauty, and we're hooked. We've started to fall.

When we have chosen an object for our passion, such as a great mind, the desire to include that object of beauty as part of the self, if intense enough, can lead to the emotion of falling in love. We have to let every barrier we have built up come down, so that we can be fully exposed to the object of our passion.

The experience is beautiful because we fall, not because the object of our passion raised us up. We have the sense of abandon in us; we fall. The expression 'falling in love,' is appropriate and very beautiful. No one ever talks about standing up in love or climbing in love or sitting in love, because always, when we fall, a deep experience of love can happen within us.

The beauty of our love affair is not in what the other person gives us or what they do for us. The beauty is in the emotion that it generates within us. The beauty is in the boundary walls collapsing around our psyche. Our mind opens and lets another life inside.

Once it happened... Jacob O'Mally fell from his second floor apartment building. When he fell, he hurt himself. People gathered around him and asked, 'Did the fall hurt you?' He replied, 'No, you idiots. It wasn't the fall that hurt. It was the stopping'.

Physical Intimacy

On a basic level, we usually want to be physically close to the object of our passion. We want proximity to the source of our love affair. We want to spend time in their physical presence. We want to physically touch them, to hug them and embrace them.

Love for a child will manifest in the desire for hugging close to the body. Sexual love usually happens through intercourse. Sex is simply the desire to merge and become one with another person. It is the ultimate in physical intimacy. However, we quickly realise that union through sex or physical proximity is limited, and cannot maintain the all-inclusive boundless emotion in the long-term. Physical intimacy is limited because it is a constant reminder that we are separate entities and that the emotion of oneness cannot usually be sustained in this way indefinitely. The body, by its very nature, is an exclusive being.

Emotional Intimacy

Falling in love is emotion-driven when the mind gives up its ties to reason. Emotional intimacy is an experience of love transferring between the self and the other. This transference then generates an exhilarating rush to the mind – one of inclusiveness. The process of transforming from a passionate experience for a specific object to a more generalised compassionate experience is that we don't just see one body as beautiful; we begin to see all bodies as beautiful. Similarly, when we fall deeply enough in love, we don't just love one mind, we love the very nature of mind itself – the nature that everyone possesses. When our emotion becomes generalised in this way, we connect to emotional intimacy in every living being and within every environment.

Mental Intimacy

When we are in love with a specific person we begin to share our thoughts. When we are more intimate we begin to share ideas. According to Plato, the world of ideas is more real than the world of stimuli. We can take in an imprint of another object or person or place and make it our own. We can hold it in our minds and be with that object of our desire. Mental intimacy can generally happen through the sharing of our thoughts and ideas, but it can also happen when we have an experience from the base of our minds, from our awareness. When we are aware we feel a mental intimacy with nature and with all other lifeforms.

Exercise – Finding Beauty

Find out what you consider beautiful in another person. Are you attracted to a person's face, hair or the shape of their eyes? Are you attracted to their height or body shape? If you are attracted to these qualities in a person then you find the physical attributes more beautiful than any other.

Are you attracted to a person's thoughts and ideas? If so, then you are more attracted to the mind of a person.

Are you attracted to a person who has intense emotions? Someone who is loving or someone who is compassionate? If so, then you find the emotion in that person most beautiful.

Devotion – A Dimensional Shift

When we take the next step from falling in love we can move into devotion. The emotion of love takes over and the world looks and feels different. The colours shine differently, we notice the beauty of existence. We see the splendour of life in the small happenings from moment to moment. When we make ourselves devout, something larger happens to us.

The most generous thing that we can do in life is to live to our peak and to set an example to the rest of the world that there is a way to live beyond all limitations. Sparing life for tomorrow is not generosity. It simply means that we are so stingy that we cannot love totally, laugh totally, or be joyful totally. We are a miser on all levels! Devotion means we are not a miser – we are full of juice! Everything in us is flowing out all the time. A devotee is seeing how to expend their life as rapidly and as fully as possible, not somebody who is trying to conserve life; not somebody who is planning to live for tomorrow. A devotee is somebody who is living now. Living absolutely.

Devotion is not a love affair. It is a much crazier happening. Love itself is a crazy thing, but there are shreds of sanity attached to it; we can still recover. In devotion, there is no shred of sanity. There is no way to recover.

A devotee has the sweetest experience of life. Everybody may think the devotee is an idiot, but they are having the best time. When I say 'devotion' I am not talking about belief systems. Belief is just like morality. People who believe think there are superior to others. All that happens the moment you believe something is that your stupidity gets confident. Confidence and stupidity are a very dangerous combination, but generally we find them together. If we start looking at all the dimensions around us, we clearly understand that what we know is so minuscule that there is no way to act with confidence. A belief system takes away this problem. It gives us enormous confidence, but it does not cure our stupidity.

Devotion is not an act. It is not directed towards something, and so the object of devotion is immaterial. It is just that with devotion we have dissolved all resistance, so that life can transpire like breath. Life is not an entity; it is a force that fills every moment of our existence. Devotion is not cool; it is hot. That is because truth is something that burns.

When we experience something as far bigger than ourselves, we naturally bow down to it. We become thankful for the gift of life. We have an experiential reality of the largeness of life, and an understanding that we are an inclusive part of it. Becoming devoid of the self is the only way to fully experience love. There is no room for our psychological thoughts within the space of the larger existence. We bow down to that which is greater.

Devotion is a way of transforming our emotions from negativity to pleasantness. People who have fallen in love do not care about what is happening in the world. We think the way they are is unrealistic, yet it is just that they have made their emotions pleasant, so their life is beautiful. That is the state of the devotee. Devotion is a multiplied and enhanced version of a love affair.

The Madness Of Devotion

If we fall in love, we become vulnerable. We don't become a devotee just because we have ascribed ourselves to a certain religion, creed or whatever. Devotees cannot ascribe themselves to anything; they are just drawn. So, before we tread such a land, we must see whether we are ready for it or not. First, you need to understand your goal. If your goal is to make life a quotient, then a very measured love affair is good. But if you are not planning to have a good life, if you want to dissolve into the process of life, if you want to become an explosion of life, if you don't care what you get and what you don't get, then you become a devotee.

A devotee is not *somebody's* devotee. Devotion is a

quality. Devotion means a certain single-pointedness – we are constantly focused towards one thing. We become receptive. Devotion means that we have the intention to dissolve into the object of our devotion. As a devotee, we don't think about whether we become a doormat or a crown on someone's head. Whatever we become is fine. Devotion is a different state of existence.

Intellect is not the problem. The problem is that we have become an exclusive intelligence, not an inclusive intelligence. Yoga, or union, means inclusiveness. To become an inclusive intelligence, so that our intelligence does not in any way distort the intelligence which is the source of creation within us, and within everything.

Conditional Love

There is really no such thing as conditional love and unconditional love, it is just that there are conditions and there is love.

Generally, we have made relationships within frameworks that are comfortable and profitable for us. People have physical, psychological, emotional, financial or social needs to fulfil. To fulfil these needs, one of the best ways is to tell people, 'I love you'. This so-called love has become like a mantra. 'Open sesame' – we can access what we want by saying these words.

Every action that we carry out is designed to fulfil certain needs. If we see this, there is a possibility that we can grow into love as our natural quality. But we can go on fooling ourselves into believing that the relationships we have made for convenience, comfort, and wellbeing are actually relationships of love. I am not saying there is no experience of love in those relationships, but the love that is experienced is within certain limitations. It does not matter how much 'I love you' has been said; if a few expectations and requisites are not fulfilled, things will fall apart. Love is a quality within ourselves; it is not something to do with somebody else.

When we talk about love, it has to be unconditional. The moment there is a condition, it just amounts to a transaction. Maybe a convenient transaction, maybe a good arrangement, but that will not fulfil us or transport us to another dimension. It is just convenient. When we experience love, it need not necessarily be convenient and most of the time it is not. It takes life.

Love is not a great thing to do, because it eats us up. If we have to be in love, we should not *be*. The expression 'falling in love' is very significant. You, as a person, must be willing to fall open. Only then can a love affair happen. If our personality is kept strong in the process, it is just a convenient situation, nothing more. We need to recognise what is a transaction and what is truly a love affair. A love affair need not be with any particular person. We could be having a great love affair with life.

What we do, what we do not do, is according to the circumstances around us. Our actions are as the external situation demands. What we do outside is always subject to many conditions. But love is an inner state – how we are within ourselves can be unconditional.

Love is never between two people. It is what happens within us – and what happens within us need not be enslaved to someone else.

Once it happened… Jacob O'Mally went fishing in his boat. After a while, something tugged on the line and he whisked it out of the water. He saw the fish had silver and gold coloured fins. It was very beautiful. He put it in the boat and the fish started thrashing for life.

Then, to Jacob's surprise, the fish spoke, 'Let me go into the river. Just put me back in the water. I will give you three wishes. You can ask for anything but put me back in the water now'. Jacob O'Mally thought for a few minutes. The fish was thrashing for life, getting weaker and weaker. Then he said, 'Make it five wishes and I'll let you go.' The fish said, 'No. Three'. Already, its voice was weak. Jacob O'Mally thought for a few more minutes and said, 'Okay, four and a half.' The fish was very weak. He said, 'No, only three. I can do only three.' Jacob O'Mally thought about this for a few more minutes before finally saying 'Okay, let's make a deal – four'. The fish didn't say anything. It was dead.

Unrequited Love

When someone we want to become part of ourselves rejects us, we experience the sting of unrequited love.

I recently stayed in a mental health facility called the Margaret Tobin centre. Dr Margaret Tobin had been shot at her Adelaide office building in October 2002 by a former psychiatrist who was found to kill out of revenge for his deregistration as a psychiatrist in New South Wales in the 1990s.

Unrequited love can be fatal. When that which we want to include as part of ourselves rejects us then we can display some powerful negative emotions. Only the loss of love and all-inclusiveness can create such powerful negative emotions.

When the psychological need for the sharing of love is not met, there is a sense of betrayal. This longing can manifest as jealousy, anger or hatred. When love is rejected, and the emotion of inclusiveness is lost, we can feel totally betrayed. Our thoughts spin back into action and, through obsessive thinking of separation, can lead into a spiralling of some dominant, damaging emotions.

Rather than see love as something that is a life condition in itself, the source of love is attributed to a specific person. In such circumstances, all it takes is for that person to 'betray' us, i.e. take away our source of love, our all-inclusiveness, and we can escalate into intense emotional reactions.

The most important point to remember about love is that the source of love does not reside within the other person or within an external situation. The source of love is generated from within, so the notion of unrequited love is essentially impossible.

Emotional Heights

Feeling alive is what most of us live for. For some people, feeling pleasant is enough. For others it's feeling exhilarated. For others still, it's a more intense emotion such as bliss. When we don't feel bliss (as a result of the psychological drama in our heads), we desperately cling to any heightened emotion – usually depression. Even though it is dull in nature and texture, its sting is sharp to the mind. It gives us a buzz of intensity. The mind cannot be still with depression. It takes a lot of energy to think depressively. It's a psychological heavyweight that needs to be pushed uphill constantly. Depression is another form of being 'high'. The emotion of depression tries to take us as far away from boredom and ordinariness as possible, but it paradoxically brings us closer to it. I have spent many months trying to sleep away the day on the sofa. Depression and lethargy are like a pair of too-tight gloves.

Mania is another emotional height. Manic euphoria is close to feeling blissed out, but it's not the same. It's the mentally ill version of being in ecstasy. I felt euphoric during my manic phases, so much so that I believed I was a god. Just imagine the exultation that a god might feel and you'd be close to imagining my state of mind at that time. There's no other place for a manic to go other than to crash back down, hence the bipolar nature of emotional heights.

Keeping With Walls Down

Being open to love takes vulnerability. We are defenceless in love and to keep the defences down takes a great deal of courage and child-like innocence.

When our psyche crumbles, the logical mind is no longer at the forefront of our reality. What seemed reasonable the day before, today doesn't make any sense. Letting down our psychological structure when we are in love is very similar to going insane. We lose our grip on logic because existence is beyond logic. Being in love has the same symptoms as going insane. We lose our perspective on life and can appear unhinged. Our reality has shifted. We lose our appetite because we are energised from a different source. We don't require as much sleep. Structures in our life that were once important lose their appeal and we may leave a job, relationship or place as it is no longer significant to us anymore.

There is no greater feeling than a realisation that we are more than just our individual psyche; that we share intimacy with another person and with a greater dimension of life, that we are a fundamental fragment of existence. When we feel in love we belong to life. We experience the emotion of connectedness because we keep the walls down. And it feels absolutely fantastic!

Gods And Gurus

So why do gurus and gods exist in people's minds and lives?

The path of devotion is not for the logically minded person. Devotion is beyond reason. It is a different form of intelligence altogether.

When some people choose a god, it is simply a love affair, one in which no response is expected. Life becomes utterly beautiful because one's emotions have become so sweet. Through that sweetness, one grows.

Loving a god means we don't get caught up in physical intimacy and the flawed psyche of another human being. We skip this step and move straight towards mental and emotional intimacy. Loving life in general, through loving an omnipotent presence, can be wonderful. However, it is often hallucinatory. Unless we have a direct experience with a god we shouldn't believe in something that is not yet in our experience. If we do, we can quickly get bogged down in dogma rather than real-life experience.

In some cultures, such as India, people place their devotion in a guru. Guru means, 'a dispeller of darkness'. A guru is a yogi who has attained union through one of the paths of yoga. People use a guru as a focus for their devotion because the yogi has already traversed the path, knows the traps of the intellect and emotion, and can help guide the person through these illusory states. The path of devotion can be especially dangerous, because when we lose our sanity we need a more experienced person to help us.

I prefer to not use a god as a path for devotion, as I haven't had direct experience of a universal entity and don't want to become hallucinatory again. I do, however, have a guru. I place my devotion at his feet and dissolve my personality completely into him.

Yoga For Emotion

Look closely at the world around you and see what you would like to take in and make a part of yourself. The beginnings of a love affair starts from a psychological process of fulfilling our needs, and drawing to ourselves that which we believe is missing from inside us. See what is beautiful in this world. When we behold beauty we automatically generate feelings of warmth and generosity towards it. The emotion of connectedness flows as we foster the quality of gratitude. It is very important not to use the psychological space to create delusive or imaginary scenarios from this emotion. Just focus on the quality and texture of the emotion, and love will deepen as a natural process.

For example, if I see a beautiful mind in the world that I want to draw to me, I have the psychological need to foster beauty within my own mind. Seeing beauty in others is the first step to integrating it into ourselves and adjusting our perspective to have a realisation that all minds contain phenomenal beauty. Similarly, we may be attracted to a person who has sweet emotions. We see those and want to make them our own, not fully understanding that we also have the capacity to generate these emotions within ourselves.

Extraordinary Life

When we live life from the separateness of our own psychological space and thoughts we miss the mystery of reality; the magnificence of existence. Life as a shared experience is fantastic. Emotional all-inclusiveness is an immense feeling that takes us out of the mediocre individual mind and into the nature of life, which is much greater. The simple everyday events of life are enough because their ordinariness is experienced through the lens of emotional pleasantness.

When it comes to emotions I feel most alive when:

- I have a love affair with Life
- I am communicating about the nature of emotion
- I am aware of the interconnectedness of the cosmos
- I am laughing out loud
- am devoted to life

Making the emotions sweet through the yoga of emotion is one way to live a full and vibrant life. We don't need anything more than the extra-ordinary. Even though the path of devotion leads to insanity, this often produces moments of sanity and mental balance which is in line with our most basic of human qualities.

The Understanding

When our emotions become pleasant we call this love. When our emotions become very pleasant we call this compassion. The grace of emotion can create a state of all-inclusiveness through the technique of devotion. It requires falling in love and stripping away all boundaries from the psyche, leaving it totally bare. It is important not to intellectualise the process of devotion, as it is easy to fall into the trap of 'conditional love', especially if the love is unrequited from a specific person. Some people who use the yoga of devotion prefer to use a guru or a god as a tool to bypass the physical intimacy of love, and instead focus purely on the mental and emotional states of boundless expansion. Oneness of emotion can easily be achieved once devotion is experienced.

The Grace of Energy

Introduction

Without energy we wouldn't be able to live. We inspire and expire our breath every moment as a transaction of energy. We know little about the mystery of our breath and the heartbeat that gives us life. This grace of life, just like the force of gravity, is always on. We are constantly exposed to the nature of grace. However, whether we chose to live by grace is our decision. There are two ways to live. We can live through our own internal thought process, using logic and reason to take life step by step, or we can live by a larger dimension of life. Grace simply gives us life in all its abundance. Grace exposes us to life without favour and without asking for anything in return. Grace, when realised, gives our life an effortless flow. We don't need to struggle and strive upstream. Grace simply carries us along. If we respond with dignity, responsiveness, and lightness we can simply sit back and enjoy the ride. With grace, suffering is not inevitable, even if we do have a mental illness.

The Existence Of Gravity

If you look at life simply you will see that gravity exists in the universe. Gravity is what makes the planets orbit the stars, like the Earth orbiting the Sun. Gravity is what makes the stars cluster together into huge, swirling galaxies. Albert Einstein came up with a revolutionary idea about gravity. He proposed that gravity is what happens when space itself is curved around a mass, such as a star or a planet. Mass tells space how to bend, and space tells mass how to move. He called this *warping in spacetime*.

People have gravity, but because our mass is relatively small compared to the size of the Earth we don't notice it as much. Earth's gravity is the reason that things falls down, instead of up. Gravity is always pulling us down. When we are totally at rest, our natural position is lying down, as close to the earth as possible. As we grow older, our skin sags due to the force of gravity on our bodies. If gravity were any stronger we wouldn't be able to walk around. We would be joined to the earth like a paper clip to a magnet.

Gravity is a marvellous thing. Without gravity, the

cells in our bodies would simply fly apart. So, gravity is strong enough to hold us together, yet it is subtle enough to let us move about of our own accord.

Gravity is a living force. It exerts itself every moment of our lives, but because we take it for granted we are unaware of it most of the time. It is only when we trip and fall that we are reminded of its presence. Gravity brings all things with energy toward one another. Gravitational forces are forces of attraction. Every object in the universe that has a mass exerts a gravitational pull, or force, on every other mass. The size of the pull depends on the masses of the objects. Similarly, every person exerts a gravitational force on the people around them. However, that force isn't usually felt because people aren't very massive, unlike planets.

At one time in our history, people didn't believe in gravity. They didn't see the gravitational force, and so they couldn't believe it was real. Today, we know that gravity exists, and it explains how and why the planets move the way they do.

The Existence Of Grace

Just as gravity exists as an entity, so too does grace. It is through the existence of grace that we become fully functional human beings. Grace is the heartbeat of life.

Life exists throughout the whole cosmos, not just on Earth. Life exists in the form of stars, planets, time, space, and darkness. If we think about life on Earth for a moment, we can see that it exists by the grace of the explosive nature of our sun. It produces life as we know it in the form of nature – the mountains, forests, oceans, and land. If we look more closely at life on this planet, with its abundant flora and fauna, we can see that it comprises a phenomenal intricacy and beauty. Even if we take one aspect of life – say an ant – and look at it through a microscope, we can see its magnificent structure and design.

And then there are humans.

Just see how much detail has gone into the manufacture and evolution of a human being. We have a physical body of technological excellence. We are free to move about the planet and we are free to think whatever thoughts we like. We have the capacity to feel emotions. We have minds of extraordinary capability, minds that allow us to be conscious of our world and to understand the workings of the cosmos. We can perceive its exquisiteness and communicate this splendour through language, and other artistic expressions such as artwork, song, and dance. We are creative beings like no other life on this planet.

The biggest experience of mind we can possibly have is that of existence. We can use our minds to behold the wondrous nature of life in all its glorious detail, and we can let our mind experience this phenomenon in all its glory. When we do this, we are living with grace.

If we do not use our creativity to express the joy of Earth's wonderful life forms, then our minds begin to suffer. We become occupied with individualised thoughts, and create a separate world within our psychological space. In this way, reality becomes split. There is a reality out there in the world, and then there is a separate reality inside our heads. We feed our individual thoughts and partial perceptions until they become a living reality within us. From that moment on, the world looks tainted. We reduce life to the realm of the menial and the mental.

Mental suffering starts off as small pains of worry generated from the petty inventions of our mind, but from there it has the potential to grow into all shapes and forms of suffering. Our minds, instead of becoming ladders to the divine, have started to become manufacturers of misery.

Human beings not only have creativity as an intrinsic quality, they also have the immense capacity for compassion. It is when these two qualities work hand in hand that the existence of grace become more conscious. When we live from a place of creative compassion for the suffering of other human beings and other life forms, we exude grace. We suddenly become conscious that grace exists, despite it constantly being *on*.

The Quality Of Grace

If you look up the definition of grace you will see one way to describe it is 'undeserved favour'. Grace is there, beneath the surface of our mind, despite our refusal to acknowledge it. Relief from our mental and emotional suffering can happen despite what we do or don't do. Grace is given freely and without the expectation of anything in return.

When we allow ourselves to become available to grace, it can change our lives in an instant. Our entrenched way of thinking can be broken open by the presence of grace. We can suddenly drop our ideologies, our beliefs, our personas, and our opinions, and become open once again to the larger dimension of life.

Grace is simply seeing life the way it is and not through our distorted psychological space. Life is above and beyond our inconsequential mind's creation of thought and emotion. Life is bigger than our manufactured, individualised thought and emotion. It exists above and beyond it, yet when we become mentally ill, we believe that the whole of existence happens inside of our heads. Our mental and emotional creations become so large that they eclipse reality. All forms of mental suffering are forms of distorted reality; not seeing life the way it is.

Grace is the thread that connects us to reality and

life in all its raw honesty. There is no possibility of suffering when we are in grace. We can live, and live fully, with a free and open mind.

The mind becomes spacious when we are in grace. Worries slip off the polished interior of our minds and we are suddenly exposed to a new way of thinking. Small, individual thoughts lose their power and a unified, expansive experience of compassion takes their place. The corresponding emotion is one of bliss. We feel bliss because we are suddenly unchained from the weighty and restrictive ideas of reality that we have synthetically made in our minds. We are free to see reality stripped bare in all its simplicity and extraordinary beauty. The colours, shapes, smells, and sounds exist in purity, and are not tainted with our insignificant, inaccurate perceptions.

To be in grace is to experience bliss.

Most of us move towards grace unconsciously. We are searching for the divine, but are looking for it in a career, a relationship, a purchased product, a house or our own internal thought structures. We can approach grace in instalments, one step at a time, or we can, in an instant, experience the full grandeur of grace. The length of time it takes us to journey towards grace is up to the individual's capacity to let go of the mind's psychological needs, and to 'ungrasp' the inventions that bind it.

Grace can wipe out the existence of our emotional traces, which can make the mind feel new again.

Youthfulness

The quality of the mind is eternally young. The mind cannot age. It is only in the physical body that ageing occurs. The mind can deteriorate or get damaged due to disease or injury, but even in that damage, youthfulness can be maintained. Youthfulness emanates a certain buoyancy and lightness within the mind. It is when the mind maintains a quality of newness and freshness.

The psychological space is the part of our mind that accumulates all of our history and memory, and can turn that history and memory into imagination about perceived futures. We have a choice. We can consistently feed this space with our attention, or we can let the past rest and see it for what it is – something that is no longer alive. To continue to engage with thoughts that are dead is to live in a state of unreality.

If we reside for long periods in our psychological space then we feed something that is no longer real. We are living a lie and are regurgitating that which should have no value. When we continue to engage with past memories, as though they were still alive, we have to continue to live with the consequences.

When we become ill, we are living in our psychological space more than in reality. Our perceptions of reality become so distorted that we physically manifest illness in our system. Usually, illness is generated by our unwillingness to let go of the past. We desperately cling to it and won't let our lives move on into the present moment. We're stuck in the past or in an imagined future that is based on past events.

Many people with mental illness contract the disease at a young age. Their minds are still forming and maturing, yet something has gone wrong. Many times, the chemistry in our brains is affected and needs external medicine to correct this imbalance. However, we can also change our chemistry using our own internal self-healing process.

One action we can take to help facilitate getting well is to 'drop' all our mental baggage. We can't actively think our way out of our tired thoughts, because to do so would be to add more thinking to our minds. Instead, we change our focus and shift the direction of our energy away from our psychological space. We start to look outside our small heads. We can use a number of techniques to let go of our psychological drama. We can focus on the breath, on other people, on nature. When we empty out our psychological stuff we make room for a more spacious mental experience. This then generates equivalent positive emotional experiences.

Imagine that your mind is like a projector in a dark room. It projects images onto the screen. As individuals, we can spend our whole lives in this dark room, watching the drama that is played out inside our minds. This is not life. Life is outside of the dark room. Outside, nature is growing and the sun is shining, but inside our dark room we believe that we have created our own reality. All that needs to happen to stop the projection of the image onto the screen is for us to raise our hand to block the transmission. Suddenly, there is no more action on the screen. We can see it for what it is, a mere projection of ideas, thoughts, opinions, and beliefs.

When we are being youthful in our minds, we simply switch off the projector inside of our dark room and walk out into the light. We breathe fresh air again and see reality in the brightness of the light. All that has happened in that projector room was merely a play of images and sounds. Nothing more. What looked like a tragedy on screen was in fact a story; a well-constructed story, but nonetheless a story that we kept engaging with by replaying it over and over again.

To be youthful is to be childlike. Children don't mull over the past. They are firmly rooted in the present moment. They don't hold onto old grievances or upsets. Even if they fall and hurt themselves physically, they are up and about with a smile in no time at all.

To be youthful in our minds is to be optimistic and open about the future. Whatever challenges we face ahead of us, we can face them better when we are in a state of youthfulness. Reclaim your youthfulness today by making a decision to live in the reality of the world, rather than in the unimportance of your own creation. It may look, feel, and taste like a real phenomenon, but our mental creations are just perpetuated illusions that contain no existential truth.

Emotional Release

It is such a simple experience to leave our mental baggage behind us, and to step out into the fresh air of reality. It can take but a moment and can have immediate transformative effects. It doesn't need to take a lifetime of mental suffering to finally figure it out. It can be dealt with in an instant. It really is that simple.

However, most of us struggle to let go of the past or the imagined, dreaded future. We grasp onto it so tightly that we cannot see any space between our true identity and the identity of our false perceptions. They seem irrevocably stuck together. When we become pathological, the very chemistry in our brains is altered and cannot be changed back so quickly.

One of the main reasons why we are so reluctant to let go of the content in our psychological space is because of the emotions we feel. Emotions are generated from our thoughts, but have a wider turning circle. We can change our thoughts almost immediately, but our emotions do not change so quickly. They take a while to build up and they stay for a lot longer than our initial thoughts. We can hold onto emotional baggage for many years through sub-conscious ideas, beliefs, opinions, and cultural mindsets.

Thoughts are like the dry kindling, and emotions are the juicy fire. Emotions can burn us up with their intensity, whether they be sadness and despair, or elation and euphoria.

What to do with our unpleasant emotions? We could use psychology to analyse the core thoughts that once generated or continue to generate the emotions. This can sometimes take years of therapy, and there is a danger that a person becomes stuck in the cycle of validation for their emotions, which perpetuates them further. For example, 'I was abused as a child' generates the intense feeling of despair that a forty-year-old is living with. Through therapy and uncovering all the in-depth details of the abuse, the emotion becomes validated as an appropriate sentiment. Relinquishing the emotions can only occur by the giving up of the thoughts that generate them. That means letting go of the past as something that no longer exists in today's reality. This includes letting go of the painful emotions that go along with them.

Letting go of emotions can feel as though someone is ripping your skin from your body. It can be that raw and painful. Our familiar emotions are our constant companions (sometimes for years or decades) before we realise that they serve no purpose other than being major contributors to our illness. Sadhguru, my guru, says that emotions have the power to change our body's chemistry. Negative emotions can have a direct impact on our physical and mental health.

The best way to move forward with emotions is to feel them, fully, without fear. One way of feeling the emotions fully is to sit with them without distraction and to breathe through them. Emotions are a shadowy presence. The fear of feeling the emotion is always far greater than the actual experience of the emotion itself. It is the emotion of fear that haunts us and gives us that sense of dread and foreboding. Rarely is the emotion associated with a memory worse than the emotion of fear that we have replaced it with.

Emotions are a deeply personal experience. Many artists have tried to capture their nebulous quality. They can colour and drain the most youthful of lives. Most negative emotion is associated with a distortion of love. Love is the desire to include something that is not you as part of you. As human beings we long for the same emotion – the emotion of all-inclusiveness. When our psychological need for this is not met, through some form of painful rejection, we can respond using defensive, damaging emotions. At first the emotions may appear like a safeguard against getting hurt again, but in the long term they become our prison and shut us out from our experience of youthfulness.

When we feel separate from the emotion of all-inclusiveness we feel isolated. We feel special because we feel we are different in some way. The emotional ego identity is born, and perpetuates its 'walking wounded' nature until we finally realise that we need to let go of this 'specialness'. For the mind, giving up our specialness (because we are the only ones who feel this way) is one of the hardest tasks.

When we are living from a perspective of separation from reality and from the all-inclusiveness of existence, we live without grace. Grace becomes a stranger to us because we have gone it alone. We suddenly have a job to do – to manage our emotions alone. It becomes a burden and, depending on how it is fostered, can develop into more heavy encumbrances as time goes on because we unconsciously set up experiences that validate that we need to hang onto this emotion of separation. To be emotionally open means that we have to become vulnerable, but we are not willing to put ourselves into such a dangerous, compromising situation.

Our emotions can seem like towering walls in front of us. This is not a constructive way to view emotions. Rather than see them as a wild, oceanic force pounding against the shoreline, we can simply let the imagery drop away and breathe with life. It is only with the recognition of our own life force that can we acknowledge other life in existence. We cannot be with life when we live in our confined, psychological space.

So how to foster the emotion of all-inclusiveness once again? The reality is that our natural emotional state is one of inclusiveness. We don't need to 'do' anything to get somewhere or add something more to our personas. Only by removing the gunk of what is there can we at last see we have been capable of experiencing this emotion all along. It never went anywhere. It was only covered by our own internal emotional baggage.

When we refer to grace we are referring to the truth that we are emotionally whole. We are not split or fragmented from reality. We never left that emotional state to begin with. It is there, but it is simply hidden by our own trifling mental creations. When we dissolve our emotional baggage, what remains is the youthful experience of grace – an all-inclusive emotion that feels like bliss.

No Conclusions

Most people have some sort of plan for their life. They have a formed identity and persona that dictates what they should wear, what they should eat, how they should exercise, where they should work, what hobbies they should engage with and so on. Each of us has a life plan, whether we are conscious of it or not.

Some people are fatalistic, believing that life has a plan for us and that we have no control over where our lives are headed. Life has no plan for us. Life simply exists. There is no universal life plan. What we make of life is our own doing.

People can be in long-term misery and life will still go on unaffected. Life is what we make it. Simply that. We can carry around emotional scars and mental suffering for as long as we want. Life doesn't prevent this from happening. We only have to look around the world and see the suffering that people experience to realise the truth that suffering happens despite life's best responses.

When we are stuck in pain and suffering, we need

help. But when the pain and suffering is happening internally, inside of our heads, without external stimuli, we can feel trapped in our own private world. Help, in whatever form it comes, can't penetrate us.

Grace, without expectation of something in return, is the only thing that can penetrate our agony. This is why it is called grace. It is undeserved favour. It doesn't request anything in return. It is a momentary relief from our suffering. A voice of sanity inside of our insane minds.

We need to be constantly aware that life has no conclusions. It is open-ended. When we live a life without making up our own conclusions, we can let life flow and carry us along to our ultimate nature. It is only by reacting against life and its process that we get stuck. We dig in our heels, telling ourselves that life should happen the way we want it to. When it doesn't go our own way, suffering is inevitable. We would like to think that the construction inside our heads is more powerful and more forceful than life itself, and it may take many years for us to be mauled by life before we finally give in to the larger dimension of life.

The larger dimension of life will happen regardless of what we think. We can only do our best in life. We can strive for our goal of all-inclusiveness, but at some point, we have to hand over to the larger dimension of life and know that external influences are mostly outside our control. We can only do so much.

We are all searching for the experience of bliss, it is just that we search for it in different places. Some go to a bar and search for it in an alcoholic drink, others prostrate themselves before a temple. Different activities with the same goal. Some of us think that having a certain career will bring forth the experience of bliss, whilst others think having a family will complete them. When we realise that every action and structure we have set up in our lives is an attempt at achieving bliss, we can realise that what we've done hasn't worked. We have been looking in the wrong place and performing the wrong activities.

Any conclusions we come to about life are bound to be incomplete or downright incorrect. By living with our incorrect conclusions, we can easily live by frustration, dejection and depression as a motivator to move around in this world, which will only end up working against us and causing more misery.

There is no need to come to conclusions about our lives. We can take one day at a time and live fully within that one day. We can strive to do our best, but then we let the consequences go. We don't become attached to the fruit of our actions. We act in the best possible way, and then surrender.

Surrender

Complete surrender is not the same as dejection. Surrender is a willingness to give up our small petty conclusions in order to live fully with life. We know that we are another piece of life and that life will always work towards fulfilling its ultimate nature, whatever that may be.

However painful it may sound, we need to surrender to life and that includes surrendering to our mental illness. Surrendering to our mental illness is not the dejected resignation of defeat. It is simply accepting the reality of the situation that we do, at this moment in time, have a disease. It is only by surrendering to our reality are we able to let go of the resistive emotions that are holding us back.

We can have a mental illness and not suffer with it if we become aware. We can surrender to grace and let our nature take its course, accepting that mental illness is happening to us. When we step into our mental illness with awareness and surrender, we let go of our emotional grasping.

When we are told we have mental illness, for some people, it can sound like a lifelong curse. Mental illness, we are told by many different sources, is a long-term illness. This means that it's with us for a while. So, while it is with us, we can either surrender to the process and live with emotional clarity, or we can become emotionally isolated and fear the illness.

Change can only come through the process of surrender. Paradoxically, it is only in giving up our idealised healthy personas that we can begin to heal. Many of us create resistance in our body's system by the refusal to acknowledge mental illness. Doctors are constantly facing an uphill battle over medication compliance because people refuse to fully accept their illness.

Being in total surrender is one of the most freeing experiences we can have. We give up our need to control the illness and the situation. We let the life within carry us along on its current. Whether or not we surrender, we will be carried downstream. It is just a matter of whether we go willingly or unwillingly.

Being unwilling to the process of life is tortuous. When we engage with the life within and around us we can do it willingly or unwillingly. One way we are motivated and give allowance to the process, the other way we are dragged kicking and screaming.

Having dignity is about doing our best in any given situation, then gently surrendering to the greater power of life.

Gentleness

Most people would baulk at the idea of doing violence to our minds and bodies, yet when we get angry or hateful at our mental illness, this is exactly what we are doing. We need to constantly be reminded to be gentle with ourselves and with our mind.

If we approach our mind as if it were a child, we will automatically have patience with it. If we flog it and berate it, all it will do is get more fearful and out of control.

Gentleness is the most soothing of balms for the mentally weary. Don't take it for granted that your mind can withstand the harshness of illness. It often can't. That is why it can appear broken. When the hard and bitter winds of mental illness are howling around your mind, grace quietly exists beneath the surface. It does not exert force, as its intrinsic nature is gentleness.

So much in this world requires applied force in order to make it work or to move. Yet grace requires no such friction. It is so subtle that it doesn't cause any disturbance at all. It doesn't add to the noise of mental illness; grace exists in the silence that is left behind after disease has waged its war. Mental illness can appear as harsh, abrasive, and painful to the psychological space. It rasps against its walls, creating inexpressible misery.

Trapped in a private, individual world of pain, grace gently seeps under the door. It remains with us even though we are entombed for what seems like forever. Grace is the one quality that doesn't leave us alone, even though we believe we are isolated. It works gently to open the door in our minds to free us from our internal suffering.

The quality of gentleness waits patiently until we are ready to experience it. It is like a mother soothing the brow of a disturbed child. That tender touch on the forehead calms our troubled thoughts. The manic panic of thoughts can be quietened by the presence of grace.

Acceptance And Responsibility

I was travelling on the bus yesterday when a man fell to the floor of the bus, having a seizure. He thrashed around on the ground groaning and making high pitched sounds. The people sitting closest to him didn't know what to do, so they did nothing. After a couple of minutes of watching another human being in the throes of suffering, a couple of people finally got up and attended to him. The ambulance was called and the paramedics gave him first aid.

Mental illness is not a choice. It just happens, like epilepsy. No matter how much willpower we have, if we have mental illness, we have it. There's very little we can do to change it.

Acceptance of our disease is the first step towards recovery. Without accepting our sickness, we can't begin to recuperate. It is at this time that we may curse grace for abandoning us to such a sequestered condition.

We don't fully understand the reasons why we get sick. Why do people live with delusion and hallucination? Why do others live in such misery or mania? We can spend a lifetime blaming certain conditions, such as genetics, our environment or ourselves, but the reality is we don't know why mental illness strikes some people with such intensity, and not others.

Ultimately, we just have to face up to our condition and accept it completely. Even though it is hard to accept mental illness as part of our identity, we have to be truthful and honest about what is happening. Blaming external sources will not help the situation. We need to become 100% responsible for our disease, and that starts with us being open with ourselves.

If we don't take responsibility for our disease, then we will never be able to move forward. We will be stuck in passing the responsibility onto our parents, our psychiatrist, our god, or whatever else you may personally want to blame. Being responsible for our illness is a huge undertaking. It means we are accountable for our own health. Others may help us, but the responsibility is firmly placed at our feet.

Whatever genetics or lifestyle we have is our lot in life. We can't do anything to change our genetics, but we can make some changes to our lifestyle. We can help ourselves by accepting we have the disease, and then taking responsibility for it. It is only by taking full responsibility that we can begin to respond to our illness in the most appropriate way. The first step to responding is by totally and completely accepting it. When we are graceful in our acceptance, we open the door of reality, even if it is just a tiny bit.

Once it happened... Jacob O'Mally parked his car and went into the supermarket. He was planning to go in for just five minutes. He went in, but then he met a friend and it took a little more time. When he came out, he saw a motorcycle police officer writing a parking ticket. He went up to her and he said, 'You pencil-neck idiot, why are you writing a ticket?' The police officer just looked at him and started writing a second ticket for bald tyres. Jacob O'Mally abused her again. The police officer wrote another ticket for expired tax. Jacob O'Mally abused her again, and she wrote another ticket.

This went on for a full twenty minutes until his friend pulled him away and asked, 'What are you doing to yourself?' Jacob replied, 'My car is parked around the corner'.

It is all about acceptance and responsibility. We include that which we think we're responsible for, and shun that which belongs to others. The secret is to take responsibility for both ourselves and others.

The Mind's Misery Manufacturing Machine

When we are in misery, we are consumed by emotion. The emotion fills us up completely until we are submerged beneath it. When we are lost in our own private torture, with the untold misery we have caused to ourselves, it looks like an impossible situation. There appears to be no way out.

Grace offers us a release us from our suffering. It is the first step in climbing out of the well we have built for ourselves. The existence of grace means we aren't damned forever in a downward spiral. We have the means for relief.

There are many forms of mental illness. I am prone to schizophrenic delusions, hallucinations, paranoia, mania, and depression. When I am experiencing these symptoms I definitely need medical and psychiatric help. I need to take medicine for my disease. During this time, I am trapped in my mind's escalating, turbulent thoughts, and my emotions drown me.

Yet, even while these symptoms are happening, I need not suffer. It is by the power of grace that I can put a little distance between myself and my racing thoughts. A little space between the avalanches of emotion.

Suffering can only happen when we become identified with that which we are not. We are not our minds. We are more than our minds. Our mind has been made up of impressions and sensations that have come through external stimuli. We have gathered our thoughts from the outside. What you gather from the outside can be yours, but it can never be the intrinsic nature of you. What is in your mind is yours, but it is not you.

Grace comes in all forms in the alleviation of suffering. It can come in the form of an ambulance, a psychiatrist, and the intake of medicine. It can come in the form of a friend. It can come in the quiet calm that penetrates through the midst of misery. Even if you are alone right now, grace is coming to you in the form of this book. And above all, there is nature.

We can never be in too much despair or suffering for grace to touch us.

Being Nothing

When the mind races of its own volition, it can sometimes be hard to think of becoming nothing. Thoughts spin around, making us sick. Emptying ourselves of our thoughts in order to create the space that allows grace to enter is the next action we can take.

Becoming empty of our psychological space can seem like an insurmountable task. The world that we have created inside of our mind seems too real to dismantle. The more we think about dismantling our interior realm, the more energy we give to it and the more real and compacted it appears.

One technique to quieten the mind is to shift the focus from our thoughts to our breath. By consciously breathing in deep, long breaths we can slow the mind. There is a direct connection between thoughts and the breath, and we can impact one by changing the other. For example, if we watch a horror movie, our breathing becomes quicker and shallower. If we are sitting amongst nature and intensely watching a leaf on a tree, our breathing automatically slows. Our breath is very subtle, so it is too easy to miss the connections between our breathing and our minds, but it is there.

Besides doing breathing exercises, any form of physical activity can quieten down the mind and take the focus away from our racing thoughts.

When we become nothing, we lose our identity to mental illness. We are not glued to it anymore. We simply drop the attachment and entanglement we have created and the mind calms of its own accord.

Emptying ourselves of our own self-importance is vital. The self-importance of our minor thoughts and emotions are but a small happening in the larger reality of existence. We need to put our suffering into perspective. In the grander scheme of things, we are such a speck of nothingness. Levelling down our own self-importance to its rightful place is one way to ensure that our interior world doesn't get too full-blown.

When we are too full of our own ego, there is no room for grace. It doesn't impose itself upon our own creations, no matter how trivial they are. It waits on the sidelines until we are ready to invite it in. However, we can't invite it in if we're too full of ourselves. Becoming nothing but a simple outcrop of life on this planet enables us to breathe freely. We can shed all our personas and excrete the misery manufacturing thoughts from our minds. We can let them dissolve away rather than making them into enduring, solid figments of our imagination.

Forgiveness

Forgiveness is required when we realise how much of a stuff-up we have made of our own minds. Through the unconscious process of our genes, or through ignorance or active misuse, we have created untold mental suffering for ourselves.

Whilst it is our intention to become nothing in the mind, we quickly come to a block and can go no further until we have learnt how to fully forgive ourselves. When we are mentally ill we can behave foolishly and think all sorts of random, bizarre, and inappropriate thoughts. It is these that we need to forgive.

In religious communities, Christianity is popular because of a man who, even when nailed to a cross, said 'forgive them for they know not what they do'. When people live by their humanity they never become bitter, angry or hateful. Regardless of what life throws at them, sometimes one tragedy after another, they rise above things. What the world throws at us is not 100% our choice, to some extent we can control it, but the world may throw anything at us. We don't know what it will throw at us. It may throw disease, it may throw death, it may throw bullets, it may throw shame. Many things may be thrown at us, but what we make out of these things is 100% ours. It doesn't matter where we go – heaven or hell – because whatever is thrown at us, we know we will turn it into wellbeing.

When we bow down to other people, it is this quality that we are venerating. If we look at Jesus' life, it is tragic. Being nailed to a cross at the age of thirty-three does not seem to represent a successful life. And yet we bow down to him because he asked that those responsible for his crucifixion be forgiven. For that we bow down to him. Not because he was crucified, but because he did not lose his quality.

It doesn't matter whether he existed or not. It's simply that people like this are an inspiration. It is the quality that matters. We recognise these qualities as great qualities. In some way we are trying to emulate them, to whatever extent we can.

So, to forgive, even those who trespass against us, is one of the worthiest qualities that humanity can have. It isn't what our forgiveness does for other people, it is what our forgiveness does for us. It releases us from our chains of bitterness, anger, and hatred. We do not resent life or people or ourselves any longer. By being gentle, we loosen up our aggrieved grip on life and learn that forgiveness is a quality that can aid us in becoming whole-minded.

Gratitude

When we are in the throes of mental illness there appears little to be thankful for. We are caught in intricate webs of suffering that layer on top of us one after the other. Many of us have had challenging lives and have faced many hardships. Why on earth should we be grateful for that misery and suffering? It is not for the suffering we give thanks. It is for the phenomenon of the mind and the majesty of its capabilities, regardless of its faults. Even if our head is in delusion and hallucination, there is still a part of our mind that can be clear. It is for this that we are grateful. It is for the respites we get between relapses that we are grateful. We are grateful for the grace of energy itself. Without it, we wouldn't exist. We wouldn't be aware and alive. We become grateful to be part of humanity, grateful that we are physical beings with mental and emotional bodies which can elevate us to great heights. We forget that the gift of life is precious. When we begin to appreciate our unique experience on this planet, then we can bow down to life itself and be grateful that we are a part of it. Never before have we lived in such a time and space, and we will never live it again.

Openness

The only way to be consistently open to the newness of life is to trust in it. Each moment takes a renewed level of trust that life is happening the way it is meant to. We can become a willing participant in this process or we can be dragged along under the current. The choice is ours. Either way, we are heading into each new day. How we enter it depends entirely upon our decision to trust and be open. We can embrace life or we can reject and resent it. Life has surprises if you let it lead you along. Magnificent happenings can eventuate, beyond our inconsequential thought process. Yet we can't be aware of life and its magnitude if we aren't open to it.

Openness takes tremendous courage. It is so easy to live closed-up in fear. It takes guts to open up and live from our heart's energy. One heartbeat at a time. One breath at a time.

Yoga For Energy

All that moves exhausts itself eventually. Only that which is still is for always.

If our mind cannot keep still, then this is an illness. We honour the energy inside us when we learn how to become still for periods at a time. Grace is a blessing because if we want to suck the sap of life we need to develop the art of stillness. When we acknowledge our energy as the purest force within us, we begin a process of healing. It only takes an instant for this to suddenly happen. When it does, it bursts forth as an emotion of bliss and ecstasy. The life within us blossoms and unfurls into something beautiful beyond our wildest imaginings.

To begin the process of accepting grace into your life, simply invite it in. Simply sit and smile, knowing that grace is not something that has to come from far away. It is present, here and now at this moment in time and space. Be with your breath, be with your heartbeat, and open up to the presence of the grace within your life. Grace doesn't require that you actively *do* anything in order for it to function.

Extraordinary Life

Life is extra-ordinary if you let it be. Just let one day happen, without resentment, without rejection, and without anger or bitterness. Just one day. Try to inspect life more closely. Look around and take pleasure in the detail of life. Simply exist here as a piece of life. Don't actively try to be different. Know that who you are right now is enough for the life beating within you.

Don't think for one moment that grace leaves you on your own. You are always in the presence of grace, so you always have an opportunity to experience wholeness and oneness at any time. There are many aspects to life that go beyond the rational and logical parts of the mind. It is not the fact that we experience a reality which is not generally accepted by other people. The problem is because we *suffer* it. If there were no suffering, there would be no problem, but because we suffer we seek help.

Don't be afraid to ask for help. There are doctors, mental health nurses, and psychiatrists who are all there to help with your medical needs. I have closed my eyes and looked inward towards my own insanity to discover what works for me. It has shown me that there is life beyond mental illness, and that you can have an experience of wholeness and fullness even if you have been diagnosed with a serious mental condition. You *can* experience blissfulness and wellbeing.

We exist as a throbbing piece of life, in harmony with the life around us. We need do nothing to realise our full potential. We already exist in unity with our body, mind, emotion, and energy. We do not need to do anything more to live well on this planet. If we fully accept our current condition and take complete responsibility for our own wellbeing, we can surrender to the process of life. We can let our petty mental creations dwindle until we become nothing more than a willing participant in life. We can begin to feel grateful for our breath, for our body, for our emotion, and for our mind. They are extraordinary gifts that can become ladders towards experiences of wholeness and spaciousness. When we begin to experience this, we witness our minds becoming youthful again. We lose the excess heavy baggage that we have dragged around in our minds. We get an emotional release, and we can feel more complete and at one with the world and ourselves.

You are not walking a path that others have not already walked down. You can be confident in knowing that others have gone into the realms of mental illness and have survived it. Not only have we survived it, but we have become wiser despite – or because of – the wounded experience we have lived through. We are touched by our own compassion, and the compassion of those who have helped us. We have suffered, survived, and risen together.

And now grace… when we have seen all of the things that we thought were the road to happiness, and discovered that they are not, now compassion and grace.

Part Four

Touching The Divine

The final section of this book will attempt to explain my recent experiences in meditation. They cannot be communicated in a linear, rational way, therefore, I have resorted to the ancient art of poetry to express the inexpressible.

May you too know the bliss of yoga. May you too be inspired to take your own tentative steps into 'Becoming a Novice Yogi'.

Grace

From the depths of slumber
As I ascend the spiral stairway of wakefulness
I whisper:
Grace! Grace! Grace!

No matter where I go, the spotlight of my mind

Ever keeps turning on Thee;
And in the battle din of activity, my silent war-cry is
ever:
Grace! Grace! Grace!

When boisterous storms of trails shriek
And worries howl at me
I drown their noises, silently chanting to my Giant:
Grace! Grace! Grace!

In waking, eating, working, dreaming, sleeping
Meditating, chanting, divinely loving
My soul constantly hums, unheard by any:
Grace! Grace! Grace!

Grace is always present
Guiding us to higher consciousness
Guiding us all home
Grace! Grace! Grace!

The Freed Mind

The bowl of Dark space and time
Juggles all the galaxies.
Stars glide by effortlessly
In perfect orbital balance,
Cosmic rhythms
Serenading the planets

I, on Earth, think too much
My tiny brain worries
About it being a bad day

Yet, the Cosmic Dance
Is Happening Wonderfully Well
The Universe is functioning
Perfectly

My specks of troubled thoughts
Need to be put back into perspective
Because
Stars glide by effortlessly
In the bowl of Dark space and time

Goodbye

Goodbye pebbles and rocks and soil
Goodbye luscious grass and leaves
Goodbye sturdy trees
Goodbye ocean ripples
Goodbye white puffy clouds
Goodbye roads I have travelled

Goodbye spicy flavours
Goodbye clean and clear water
Goodbye chirping tweeting birds
Goodbye haunting songs
Goodbye sweet nothings
Goodbye laughter

Goodbye loved ones
Oh' your gentle natures
Goodbye loyal partner
Thank you for teaching me how to live
Goodbye foes and community
Thank you for teaching me how to live

Goodbye work and worry
Goodbye hard to come by money
Goodbye safe and secure home

Goodbye art and science
Goodbye sofa and bed and toilet

Goodbye dappled sunshine
Goodbye warm rain
Goodbye seasons
Goodbye birth and death
Goodbye mother Earth

Goodbye sad tears and hospitals
Goodbye sleepy dreams
Goodbye hairs on head
Goodbye sense-full body
Embalming me in flesh

Goodbye mind
Goodbye emotion

Goodbye breath
Hello death of suffering

Ultimately

So now you have seen my body
So now you know my emotions
So now you know my thoughts
And know my wounds and wisdom

Regardless of all,
In the ultimate I dwell

So now you know who I am
My fears and fascinations
The nebulous core of who I am
Empty yet full
Frail yet indomitable
A stranger no more

Because of it all,
In the ultimate we dwell

Just a Play

To be written last but coming first
This poem expresses the bliss of the game
The journey to inner self
Starting with suffering
Which transforms to joy
When you realise
It's all just a Play

I'm so stupid
I missed it
I'm so ignorant
I skipped it
I'm so idiotic
I delayed it

No more
No more
Will I miss it
Skip it
Or delay it

Just
A
Game

That
I
Have
Played

I Blame It on You

When I lose control
I blame it on You

When the world conspires
With magicians and music
I blame it on You

When my heart leaps and skips
And expands
To the edges of existence
I blame it on You

When my mind shatters
Disintegrates fragmented thoughts
Absorbs and includes
Oceanic depths
I blame it on You

When I am blessed
With no inhibitions
When freedom is not a word
But the sunshine on my face
And the Flower in my hair
I blame it all on You

With my partner in this delicious crime
What am I waiting for?

What You Do To Me

You are the depths
of darkness
You are the shell
of Sunlight

You fill my oceans
You craft my mountains
You make it hail and thunder
And down it pours on me

You select my stars
That shine for me

You light my sky
With your fire

You nurture my wounded nature
And care for my creatures
You feed my forests
To offer me shade
Whilst I weep by the willows

You drench me
You burn me
You bury me
You leave me

Dripping in ecstasy

Every Love Song is Sung For You

Dearest Beloved...

Every song that sings of Love
Is sung especially for you

You are the greatest lover
The most patient carer
The most loyal parent
The most devoted disciple

You created love
You branded me with it
And now I am bitten
Smitten
With you

Let us love each other
To the fullest possible heights
With this little time
We have left

Living with Grace: Conquering this World

With the power of my Guru
And the Saints and Sages
Of the centuries
I stand tall
And look beyond this world

This world has tried to
Crumple me into a ball
And kick me to the kerb

Yet through my trials and tribulations
I stand tall
And look beyond this world

For every piece of strife
I have taken the shot and
Fed the mud to my Lotus

Dear companions
Thank you for your company
On the road to Damascus
It has led me here
To this point in time
At this location

And I couldn't think of any better place to be

Ambassadors of Yoga:
Living with Grace

The Masters of Yoga:
Yogananda, Sadhguru, Krishna and Shiva
Are giants amongst men

Yet here I am
A tiny pathetic voice
Speaking up for a tradition
That I know little about

How can I speak up
For the science of yoga
When I am so flawed?

Yet, I want to get my message
Out there that
Yoga has changed my life

How can I speak
For the science of yoga

When I am so defective?

I want to fulfil
My master's plan
That all beings are touched
By the power of yoga

I am ashamed that I
Can't be a better ambassador...

Living with Grace: Reveal Thyself!

Immersed in my teacher's convocation
I hear the silent whisper
From Eternity
Reveal Thyself!

Painter of nature
Creator of trees
Lord of the human race
Reveal Thyself to me!

Too long have you been

Hidden from my sight
Long has my journey been
In search of Thee

Just as I know you are the
Author behind my words
So too you prick
My Consciousness

Reveal Thyself to me
Oh' Lord of the Divine Play

Living inside the Mind of God

The tiny bubble of my mind bursts
And I find that I am still inside a Mind
An inclusive Mind that encompasses All

God, God, God
Throbs in my ears
Is in my mouth
Are my eyes

My creator and the creator of All

Sings me a sweet melody
'I have revealed my Creation'
In awe I inspect the Ant
And look up at the night sky
So much detail
Such a phenomenal intelligence

Then there's me
Little old me fumbling in the cupboard
I chanted 'Reveal thyself'
And the joke was
He was in every pore of my skin
In every shade of light falling on my eyes
He has always been there

My Creator Has a Sense of Humour

A mustard seed -
The universe in a mustard seed
I pop it into my mouth
But do not swallow

How does liberation knock on my door?

Little old me
Incognito, insignificant, ordinary me
Humbling emotions engulf me

In all these years of searching
He remained Unseen
In all these years of suffering
He kept silent

No, it was I who kept silent
Gradually growing more soundless
Listening instead of talking
Knowing the suffering to be my own making

I couldn't meet Him eye to eye
I rejected Him
I abandoned Him
I Hated Him

My hatred became my own demon
Festering the wounds within
Tipping the scale of sanity towards insanity
Until all I sought was comfort
But I knew comfort wasn't getting me there

Prayer didn't work for me

Devotional whisperings do
They wore away at my hatred and disgust
I kept whispering to the wind
'Let me Meet my Maker'
In earnest at first
Then in light-hearted instinctiveness

Until He saw that I was unwound
And casually said 'Hi' back

Infinity Guided Meditation

A declaration that the world and me are one
Is followed by my Guru's whisper
'To infinity and beyond!'

He encourages me to fall
Fall into the vast cosmic darkness
There is no bottom
No sides to graze my knees
Just one fantastic freefall

Infinity is waiting to be realised

Mountain Mover

Ocean Waver
Wind Blower
Rain Inventor
Star and planet creator
Creature maker
My Maker

Mountain Mover

Yogi Initiator
Nature Architect
Love Author
Bliss Originator
Consciousness Designer
My Maker

Mountain Mover

Reveal Thyself to me

The Inner World

My astral diamonds inner world
Sparkles in the Light
I know the language of Spirit
It whispers silently to me
'Awaken'
Come alive to the reality and truth
The beauty of inclusion
The merging of Yoga
With the Lord of Time and Space

Creation is but a pale dimension
To the inner world
Our inner world

Pain and suffering, old age and birth
Cannot exist here
Here we are liberated from the
Cycles of Birth and Death
Longing and Loss

No more to wander
In the halls of shade
We, at last, come out
Into the Light of Knowledge

Knowledge that the Christ in me
and God never parted

Bildungsroman

I am making my life
Into a Bildungsroman
Drama and thrills to start
Followed by a rom com
Then horror
Fantasy follows
All the while I am
Shifting and growing
Sideways

Until the touch of a blessing
Bestowed from a long
Ago treasured memory
Touches my brow
'Evolve' it whispers
'Don't be afraid
I am with you'

I close my eyes
To take the most
Frightening journey yet
Monsters and demons
Are inside
Until I realise they
Are but my thoughts
My karma

I leave them to dissolve
And move towards
The light of knowledge
At the centre of my brow
My spiritual eye

Avatars come to see the spectacle
Of a mortal in ignorance
Steeped in karma
Step through the portal
Nothing can hold me back now

Herein is the story of my life

A Bildungsroman

Let the Darkness Out

Give your darkness
To your Gurus
Leave no corner of your heart
Unturned

Every transgression
Every scrap of karma
Lay it all at your Gurus' feet

Turn yourself inside out
Expose every rip of darkness
To Thine shining eyes

Apologise
'I'm so sorry'

Let it all out
Don't hold onto anything
Let every thought
Ever thought be inspected

In the darkened room of our hearts
Let the intense light
Twinkle and illuminate

Ah' but it is all a dream

In the end
Let's make it a dream
Filled with integrity
And Humanity

Our Gurus wink at us
And let us know it is all
Going to be alright

Selfless service awaits

Turning Inward

The journey doesn't begin
Until one is sitting with spine erect
Relaxed
Calm
Mild focus on space between eyebrows
Thoughts soft and in the background

Up until this point
All is a game
A foolhardy game

Sit without distractions
Wait on the edge of infinity
(The easy edge of our mind)
Don't take yourself seriously

This is a play
A dance
A song
A poem
A love story
A Homecoming

Let the drop of a tear
Fall from our heart
In gratitude
That we are finally
On the path

Wetting our Cheeks

So many tears
Have wetted the cheeks
Of Humanity
Despondent tears
Tears of pain

So many tears
Have wetted my cheeks
Miserable tears
Tears of pain
Self-absorbed moans

Our eyes have become
Blurred and dull
We can no longer see clearly

Creation and Creator
Are lost in the jungle of
Our psyche and physicality

Endlessly, this can continue
If we don't consciously
Choose a new path
The inner guided dominion

Tears flow from my eyes
Now
Not in angst but in elation
Not in distress but in appreciation

I am moved to tears
By the Grace
Bestowed upon me
The enormity of it
Bows my head
Swells my heart
And a single glad tear
Slips down my wet cheek

Novice Yogi

I'm such a scatterbrain
Not an expert in anything
More of a dabbler
A touch here
A dash there

Knowing I am a fool
I tread the yogic path

Knowing I am a novice
I take instructions from
The Masters of Yoga

It's as simple as that!

Keeping myself aside
Emptying myself of puffed up self-worth
Thawing my resistances
And softening my likes and dislikes
I walk the path

Many others have gone before me
I open my ears and listen
To their advice
And keep my mouth shut

In unchartered terrain
It is best to take instructions
From one who is experienced
And who knows the way

I am in foggy terrain
I cannot see ahead

So I hold onto the coat-tails
Of my Master Yogi
In pure Trust

Devoted Heart

Alone, my heart swells
With the tenderness of a mountain
I feel connected
To Life and its inhabitants
Even inanimate objects are
Filled with Grace
As Divine love
Pours through me

In the company of others,
I am just another somebody
A regular person who says
Regular things
I choose not to speak about my
Pulsing heart
It is a lover's secret
Love affair

Oh' to share my tenderness
To woo your heart
So you too may
Burst with devotion

There is no other way to live
For me
The sweetness of your fragrant heart
Liquefies my being

'Speak to Me'

When you want to open your heart
Speak to me

When you are lonely at night
And it has been a long day
Write to me

When tears of desolation spill
Down your cheeks
Whisper to me

When confusion muddies your mind

And you feel you are losing it
Communicate with me

I have already walked
This path
The path of Opening the Heart
I know what it is like
To be lost

Let your yogi be the light for you
Let them take your hand
And show you the way

'Speak to me'
I am here for you

Untangled

Long I have wandered
In oblivion

You can easily get tangled up in this world
Ever new sparkly objects snag the eye
The mind spirals down the rabbit-hole

Of ever novel digressions
Our emotions get ensnared on the
Weeds of our mind;
Fear, anger, jealousy, depression

Oh how heavy the world can be
When we are entangled
In worldly activities
It is the nature of our mind
To get entangled

Now I have found a way out
A doorway
I have ensnared myself
In my Guru
I wrap myself around him
My heart is entwined with His
My very energy belongs to him

I know he is safe to
Tangle with
Because He knows
The way to the Ultimate
Not me

His promise to me
Is written in my soul

On The Path

No matter what happens
Rain, shine or hail
I am on the path

The spiritual route
Has opened before me
And I am on my way

At last, I am pointed
In the correct direction

Many yogis have
Walked this way
They have forged through
The forest of dreams
And they stand by
To cheer me on

There is nowhere else
I'd rather be than
On the spiritual Path

The Joker in a Tragedy

Each commoner a king
The foolhardy kings
With their crooked crowns
Abide in their castles

The castle walls are thick
Yet crumbling
Enemies pommel
At the moat gate

The streets are littered with human filth
And people hold their heads
To mitigate the torment
They wail in unison
'Doomsday is coming'
Bawls the town-crier

It is only the joker
Who sits in the street
Picking ticks off the wild dogs
Humming a sweet tune

Only he sees the tragedy
For what it is

Self-created

Sharing the Devotion in my Heart

Coins drop from my heart
I pick them up and give
Each one to you
In the form of a song

My heart is open
It sings to the sky
To the Creator
To my Yogi

But most of all
It sings to you

Sometimes I'm pointless
Sometimes I'm thoughtful
Sometimes I'm mischievous
But I am always authentic

I sing the same song in
A thousand different ways
Hoping to capture you
In the wide Blue net

Sharing the Devotion in my heart
Is my present to this realm

Your Move Playmate

Spiritual Master
Illuminated Yogi
Wise mystical Soul
Come play with me

You've seen me naked
And watched me go crazy
You recognise my thoughts
(My heart is already yours)
And you know what makes me laugh
Come, won't you play with me?

I place you above my head
At the top of the kingdom
I worship you
Like I would the Creator himself
Come, won't you play with me?

I can't promise to play fair
Sometimes I lie and cheat to win
Come, won't you play with me?

Here, take my hand
And let the world be our playground

Use the actors on life's stage
To write the greatest love story
Of our time

Your move playmate…

Genuine Love Never Dies

The compulsiveness of concubines
Scratching out a living
Is not the kind of love I'm talking about

The manic compulsive obsession
Of a person with handsome features
Is not the kind of love I'm talking about

The sexual intimacy of lovers
That fades in time
Is not the kind of love I'm talking about

The love of a husband and wife
That is destined to end in divorce
Is not the kind of love I'm talking about

The lure of the wounded soul
And their attraction
Is not the kind of love I'm talking about

When love flourishes and evolves
When devotion to the other
Takes over your breath
Takes over your life

When your lover has a totally open heart
When your lover is compassionate and tender
Yet honest enough to tell you the truth
When your lover has touched your soul
When your love becomes God herself

Then that genuine love never dies

The Dreamcrusher

May you have every dream crushed
By the Dreamcrusher

May your fantastical hopes
Be flattened

Dreams and delusions
Keep us from seeing reality as it is

Truth can never be found
In hallucinations
Only when every last dream
Has been stripped away
Do we see the raw truth

May you not wait for the Dreamcrusher
To come and crush your dreams
May you put an end to them yourself

What is waiting is far larger
Than you could ever dream of

In the Presence of Divinity

My creativity comes from you
My artwork channels you
And any of my innovative endeavours
Has its roots in you

Here, take my scribblings

That have arisen from my heart
Dipped in gold-leaf
They are rightfully yours

The fragrance of my heart
Smells of you
My awareness only sees your aura
Your heart is now beating in my chest

You have the whole world
At your feet
What use may I be for you?
As I abandon myself in you

How to tell the world of your identity?
And the gift you have to offer

Dear friends, we are in the company of Divinity

Fences and Walls

Just when I think, 'I am here'
Another wall collapses and I see yonder
Yet other walls ahead

And beyond the walls are fences
Penning me in

Just when I think I am empty
I open up to a new dimension
With its tethers
Still holding me down

Do I become disheartened
At the enormity of the journey?
Do I crawl back into my safe cell?
Or do I celebrate the small victory and move on?

The mind has many compartments
Many yellow brick roads
Many fences and walls

'Continue with your sadhana
It is your lifeline

I am with you'

Vulnerability to Dissolve

Such a solid personality
Full of likes and dislikes
Opinions and conclusions
Brimming with thoughts
Scrappy emotions

Can I put all this aside?
Can I be vulnerable to You?

Can I open the iron-clad door
That keeps me imprisoned inside?

One look into your eyes
And I start to disintegrate

I close my eyes
And know
You are my constant companion
Ever patiently waiting for that moment
When I will crack open
Leaving the brittle shell
Ever ready to catch me

I have a lifetime of hardness
To resolve

Lifetimes of resistance and fear
To liquefy

Do I have the courage, the trust,
The vulnerability to dissolve?

Feeling Like a New Born

In the presence of the Cosmic Mother
I bow down
And ask for her blessing

She holds me to her bosom
Just like I am a new born
And showers me with
Her unconditional love
The feeling is overwhelming
And tears drip down my cheeks

How I have longed for this love!
Finally, it is here
In this moment

I open my eyes

To see if it is still real
In the dusk of the meditation room
I see her before me

Yes, she is real

Just like the moon's surface
I have been barren of love
It has taken the cosmic mother Herself
To shine her light on me
Now I am glowing
And radiating her light

My heart has been touched... partially opened...
In the cave of my chest
Unknown treasures
From within
Await

This is Not It

Having a beautiful home – this is not it
Having a relationship – this is not it
Having money in our pocket – this is not it
Having a child – this is not it
Buying a fast car – this is not it
Eating fancy food – this is not it
Getting drunk – this is not it
Acting smart – this is not it
All forms of education – this is not it
Being creative – this is not it
Dying – this is not it
Imagination and memories – this is not it
Emotions and thoughts – this is not it
Health or sickness – this is not it
Sensations – this is not it

When you are done
With all that is not
Seek what is...

Your Light Shines In Me

Your glorious Light
Shines in me
Holding the very atoms together
Giving life-affirming wellbeing

Your intense Light
Floods in me
Being the very life-force
That I am

Your dazzling Light
Showers in me
Burning away all
Symbols of sickness

Your magnificent Light
Is a gift straight from the
Source of Creation

You
Shine in me

Dissolving Memory and Imagination

Wipe out the trauma
The agony, the same repeating mistakes
Wipe out the tears
That stain your cheeks
Wipe out the rage
With its destructive toxins

Wipe out your Loves
The heart-stringed ties
Wipe out the longing
That threatens to destroy
Wipe up the broken pieces

Wipe out the silly dreams
Of happy ever after
Wipe out the friendships
With all their bondage
Wipe out the ancestors
And their ghostly tinkering

Wipe out needing another
To lean on
Wipe out the plaque from
The veins

Grow a spine

Oh' but keep one memento
The loyalty and love of the mother to all
And the kindness of a best friend stranger
Who puts humanity to shame

Empathy for Pain and Suffering

Too much physical woe
Bodies racked by pains
People hurting
How can we not feel a connection?

So much suffering
In the mind's eye
So many cuts and sores
Festering in secret thoughts

Oh' to be responsible
For our humanity
And empathise with the weak
Letting ourselves feel what they feel

Unfriendly emotions and thoughts
Unpleasant bodily sensations
People fighting against themselves
Let us not be one more enemy

Compassion connects
Empathy unites
Let my compassion and empathy
Be a soothing, medicinal ointment

Entering the Doors of Liberation

A supportive friend
Leads me to the doors of liberation
All I have to do is enter

The entrance of oneness
Openly awaits
For my arousal
No more slumber
In the twilight zone
I roar, 'I Awaken!'

And step across the threshold

Touching Nirvana

I can stand up and fight
Or I can melt away

I can become undefeatable
Or I can surrender at Will

I can shout, 'Arise'
Or I can dissolve

I can become Everything
Or I can become Nothing

I can become God's very child
Or I can be as an orphaned ant

I will always define myself
As an empty vessel
Patiently pausing to be filled

Inward from Senses

Outward bound senses
You are but false
A restless, cosmic prison for form
An endless universe of separation
And lost disunion

This earth will never reveal the answer I seek
Nor the hidden nugget of Truth

Ah, but the moment I close my eyes
And shut down my senses
I am left only with a beating heart
A breathing heart

Tears flow
Emotions flow
And in the seed of my devotion
Inside of me
I find oneness with Divinity

All River's Flow to the Ocean

I made friends with the River last year
Intrigued by his nature
Ever-flowing and fluid
Cool yet enveloping

I sat by the banks of the River
And chit-chatted
Expressed my dreams,
My hurts and failings
I showed my puny mind
Opened my scarred heart

We conversed like dear old friends
Why do you accept me, River?, I pondered
As I peered into its depths
And
Saw him holding my reflection

A dawning...
River knew me all too well
Perhaps better than I knew myself

I too am made from water
I too am the River

We are not unconnected

A silent, joyful tear
Gently rolled down my cheek
and fell into River's depth

The last poem and word of wisdom is from my beloved Guru, Sadhguru

Empty Page (by Sadhguru)

When thoughts that are
too profound for words
form in one's mind
Heart swells, lifts tides high
The veil of time cracks and
reveals the roots of past
and what pretends as future

A man who lives through this
is no more just a man
The world will label him a sage
But in truth he is a fathomless empty page

Postscript

If you would like to talk with me about my book or any of the ideas portrayed here, please feel free to contact me via email:

emptyshiva@gmail.com

May your journey to liberation be short and swift.

About the Author

Elizabeth Owen lives and works in Adelaide, South Australia.

She is, as she says herself, a force to be reckoned with. She has one goal in this life and one goal only – to become a Yogi. Everything she does is dedicated to this single aim.

Elizabeth has lived a quiet life – that is, until the actuality of mental illness struck in 2011. She was left reeling from such an all-consuming life experience and it has taken her years to regain her equilibrium. Her mental illness has taught her some valuable life lessons – not least to live life fully and completely at every opportunity and to surrender to every moment.

Elizabeth doesn't define herself by her career or by her hobbies but by the incremental steps she has taken to becoming a Novice Yogi.

She hopes you enjoy the book, which is a journey of discovery through mental illness and beyond. Indeed, liberation and enlightenment are possible for ordinary, flawed human beings.